Enjoying Where You Are On the Way To Where You Are Going

Learning How To Live
A Joyful Spirit-Led Life

by
Joyce Meyer

Harrison House
Tulsa, Oklahoma

17th Printing

Enjoying Where You Are On the Way
To Where You Are Going
ISBN 0-89274-948-2
Copyright © 1996 by Joyce Meyer
Life In The Word, Inc.
P. O. Box 655
Fenton, Missouri 63026

Published by Harrison House, Inc.
P. O. Box 35035
Tulsa, Oklahoma 74153

Contents

Introduction

I believe that life should be a celebration. Far too many people don't even enjoy life, let alone celebrate it. I frequently say that many people are on their way to heaven, but very few are enjoying the trip. For many years I was one of those people.

God has taught me a great deal about how to enjoy life. He has showed me that the life He has given us is meant to be enjoyed. Jesus came that we might **have and enjoy life, and have it in abundance (to the full, till it overflows)** according to *The Amplified Bible* version of John 10:10. There are many other similar Scriptures in the Bible that I will expound on in this book.

I believe that reading this book may be life changing for you. Perhaps you are as I was at one time. You truly love the Lord with all your heart and are trying so hard to please Him that you are forgetting to live to the full the abundant life He has provided.

Enjoyment of life is not based on enjoyable circumstances. It is an attitude of the heart, a decision to enjoy everything because everything — even little, seemingly insignificant things — have a part in the overall "big picture" of life.

When I finally realized that I was not enjoying my life, I had to make a quality decision to find out what was wrong and rectify it. This decision demanded learning new ways of handling situations.

Once I discovered that the world was not going to change, I decided that it was my approach to some of the "lemons" in life that needed adjustment. I had heard someone say that lemons can make us sour or we can turn them into lemonade. My decision to make lemonade instead of turning sour required that I learn balance in my work habits.

I was a workaholic who found great satisfaction in accomplishment. Of course, God desires and even commands us to bear fruit. We should not waste time and be "do-nothings," but an unbalanced attitude in this area causes many people to experience burnout from a lifestyle of all work and no play. I was one of those people. Actually, I didn't know how to play and truly enjoy it. I always felt I should be working. I felt safe only when I was doing something "constructive."

I also had to change my attitude toward people. I learned that one of the reasons I didn't enjoy life was because I didn't enjoy most of the people in my life. I was trying to change them so I would find them enjoyable instead of accepting them the way they were and enjoying them while God was changing them.

I believe that all of us truly need teaching on this subject of how to enjoy where we are on the way to where we are going. I pray that this book will be a major blessing in your life, and that, as you read it, God will bring you to a crossroads — a place of decision — where you can choose to begin celebrating life.

1

Life Is a Journey

The thief comes only in order to steal and kill and destroy. I came that they may have and enjoy life, and have it in abundance (to the full, till it overflows).
John 10:10

I have come to the conclusion that there is nothing as tragic as being alive and not enjoying life. I wasted much of my own life because I did not know how to enjoy where I was while I was on the way to where I was going.

Life is a journey. Everything in it is a process. It has a beginning, a middle and an end. All aspects of life are always developing. Life is motion. Without movement, advancement and progression, there is no life. Once a thing has ceased to progress, it is dead.

In other words, as long as you and I are alive, we are always going to be going somewhere. We are created by God to be goal-oriented visionaries. Without a vision, we atrophy and become bored and hopeless. We need to have something to reach for, but in the reaching toward what lies ahead in the *future,* we must not lose sight of *now!*

I see this principle in every area of life, but let us examine just one of those areas.

Spiritual Life

Let's say an unsaved person who has no relationship with God becomes aware that something is missing in his life and so he starts searching. The Holy Spirit draws him to the place where he is confronted with making a decision about placing his faith in Christ. He accepts Him and then moves from the place of searching for an unknown something to discovering what or who that something is. In so doing, he enters a temporary place of satisfaction and fulfillment.

Please notice that I said *temporary*, because soon the Holy Spirit will begin drawing him to press on to a deeper place in God. The process of conviction of sin will begin in his daily life. The Holy Spirit is the Revealer of truth (John 14:16,17), and He works continually in and with the believer to bring him into new levels of awareness. Entering a new level always means leaving an old one behind.

In other words, we are always heading somewhere spiritually, and we should be enjoying the journey. Seeking God's will for our lives — allowing Him to deal with us about attitudes and issues, desiring to know His call on our lives and yearning to fulfill it — all these things are part of the journey of Christianity.

"Desiring" and "seeking" are words we will use frequently in this study, and both of them indicate that we cannot stay where we are. We must move on! However, this is precisely the point at which multitudes of us lose our enjoyment of life.

We must learn to seek the next phase in our journey without despising or belittling the one in which we currently find ourselves.

In my own spiritual pilgrimage, I finally learned to say, "I'm not where I need to be, but thank God, I'm not where I used to be. I'm okay, and I'm on my way!"

The spiritual struggle that most of us go through would be almost totally alleviated if we understood the principle being discussed on these pages.

The Ben Campbell Johnson relational paraphrase of Jesus' words in Matthew 11:29 gives some insight into what our attitude should be concerning our personal spiritual growth. It reads as follows: **"Take the burden of responsibility I give you and thereby discover your life and your destiny. I am gentle and humble; I am willing to relate to you and to permit you to learn at your own rate; then, in fellowship with me, you will discover the meaning of your life."**

Notice that in this passage Jesus says, **"Take the burden of responsibility I give you...."** Many of us take a responsibility the Lord has never given us. We actually try to become "Holy Ghost, Jr." Instead of allowing the Holy Spirit to work the Word in us and change us from glory to glory, or from degree to degree (2 Cor. 3:18), we try to do it on our own. We struggle so hard trying to get to the next place we feel we need to be that we fail to enjoy where we are.

We absolutely *must* realize the importance of each phase. Each phase is vital to the next one. For instance, a child cannot be two years old until he has lived each of the days between the ages of one and two. Wherever it is we are headed, we are not going to get there any faster than God takes us. We must learn to do our part and trust God to help us enjoy the journey.

I believe I change daily. I have goals in every area of my life. I desire improvement in all things. This time next year I will be different from what I am now. Various things in my life, family and ministry will have improved. But the good news is that I have discovered the soul-satisfying secret of enjoying where I am on the way to where I am going.

We might say that there is always something new on the horizon. The Lord showed me this truth in a vision almost twenty years ago as I was considering enrolling in a Bible school program sponsored by our church three evenings a week. It was a major commitment for my husband Dave and me. At the time we had three small children at home, and yet we felt God calling us to a new level of ministry. I was excited, but apprehensive.

Once we made the decision, I began to feel that this commitment would be "the thing" that would make "all" the difference in the world. It seems that we humans are always looking for "it!"

As I was considering this decision, God gave me a vision of a horizon. My husband and I were heading toward it, but as we finally came near to it, another horizon appeared out beyond the first one. It represented yet another place to reach for once we had arrived at the current one.

As I pondered what I was seeing, the Lord revealed to my heart that there would constantly be new goals out in front of us. I felt He was telling me not to think in small terms, not to become narrow-minded, not to make small plans, but to always be reaching for the next place that would take me beyond where I was. I regret to say that even though I did the reaching, and I was not complacent, it took several more years before I learned to enjoy each step of the journey.

I was always going somewhere and never truly enjoying anywhere. I was deceived by thinking that I would have joy when I arrived — that *now* was only a time of sacrifice and hard work.

I am very thankful for the Holy Spirit's patient and continuing work with me as He taught me to enjoy every aspect of my life — the beginning of projects, the middle and the finish, the people in my life, my home, myself and the ministry in which God has placed me.

Now, I am as thankful for the rainy days as the sunny ones. I am even thankful for the time I spend in the airports I wait in because I travel so much...on and on the list goes.

Once we learn the principle, we can apply it everywhere.

Jesus said that He came that we might have and enjoy life. If you have not been enjoying your life, it is time to begin. If you have been enjoying your life, thank God, and look for ways to enjoy it even more.

2

Make a Decision To Enjoy Life

I call heaven and earth to witness this day against you that I have set before you life and death, the blessings and the curses; therefore choose life, that you and your descendants may live.

Deuteronomy 30:19

In the Word of God we are exhorted to choose life. The Hebrew word translated "life" in Deuteronomy 30:19 is *chay*, and means, among other things, "fresh," "strong," "lively" and "merry."[1]

In John 10:10, Jesus said that He came that we might have life. According to *Vine's Expository Dictionary of Biblical Words*, the New Testament Greek word translated "life" in this verse is *zoe* and means, in part, "...life as God has it, that which the Father has in Himself, and which He gave to the Incarnate Son to have in Himself,....and which the Son manifested in the world...."[2]

The biblical dictionary then goes on to say, "From this life man has become alienated in consequence of the Fall,...and of this life men become partakers through faith in the Lord Jesus Christ...."

---

[1]James Strong, *The New Strong's Exhaustive Concordance of the Bible* (Nashville: Thomas Nelson Publishers, 1990), "Hebrew and Chaldee Dictionary," p. 38, entry #2416.

[2]W.E. Vine, Merrill F. Unger, and William White Jr., *Vine's Complete Expository Dictionary of Old and New Testament Words* (Nashville: Thomas Nelson, Inc., Publishers, 1985), p. 367.

The life being referred to here is not simply a span of time. It is a *quality* of existence — life as God has it. We human beings lost that kind of God-like life due to sin, but we can have it back through Christ Jesus. It is God's gift to us in His Son.

Quantity and Quality

I cannot imagine that God does not lead a thoroughly enjoyable life. To even begin to have an understanding of the quality of life that God enjoys, we must change our modern perspective of what constitutes real life.

Our society has fallen into the trap of believing that quantity is greater than quality, but this is not true. This lie from Satan has been fuel for the spirit of greed that prevails in our world today. It is becoming more and more difficult to find anything that is of excellent quality. In most industrialized nations of the world, especially in America, there is an abundance of everything, and yet there are more unhappy people than ever before.

I believe that if we had more quality and a little less quantity, we would experience more real joy in our everyday lives. It would be far better to live forty years to the fullest, truly enjoying every aspect of life, than to live a hundred years and never enjoy anything. Thank God, we can have both a long life and a quality life, but I am trying to make a point.

Here is an example: Think of fragrances. A few drops of pure perfume will smell stronger and stay on longer than a much heavier application of a more watered-down version such as cologne or eau de toilette. Real perfume usually comes in much smaller bottles and is much more expensive. The diluted versions come in larger bottles and are less expensive. Most of us automatically go for the bigger bottle with the lower price. When giving a gift, we think it looks more impressive if it is packaged in a large container.

Some of us wouldn't even know what we had if we received a present of real perfume. Because it usually comes in very small bottles, we might even think we had received a gift of little value. We might conclude that our benefactor was cheap and didn't care enough to spend more money on us, when all the time we were holding something of much greater value than we realized.

There are many examples I could use, but suffice it to say that in most things of life, quality is far superior to quantity.

As believers, you and I have available to us the quality of life that God has. His life is not filled with fear, stress, worry, anxiety or depression. God is not impatient, and He is in no hurry. He takes time to enjoy His creation, the works of His hands.

I noticed in the account of Creation as recorded in Genesis 1, Scripture frequently says that *after* God had created a certain portion of the universe in which we live, He saw that it was good (suitable, pleasant, fitting, admirable), and He approved it. (See verses 4,10, 12,18,21,25,31.) It seems to me that if God took the time to enjoy each phase of His creation, His work, then you and I should also take time to enjoy our work. We should work not just to accomplish, but also to enjoy our accomplishments.

Learn to enjoy not only your work and your accomplishments but even the ride to work in the morning. Don't get so frustrated about traffic and have your mind on what you need to do when you arrive that you fail to enjoy the trip.

Most people dread and even despise the drive home from work at night. They are tired, traffic is heavy, and they begin to think about all the things they must do, but don't want to do, when they get home — cook dinner, go to the store, cut the grass, change the oil in the car, help the children with homework, etc.

Don't do that. Learn to enjoy every aspect of your life. Enjoy your home, your friends and your family. Don't just have children, but take the time to enjoy them.

All it takes to begin to enjoy life to the fullest is a decision.

A Decision Can Change It All!

We will never enjoy life unless we make a quality decision to do so.

Satan is an expert at stealing, and our joy is one of his favorite targets. Nehemiah 8:10 tells us that the joy of the Lord is our strength. In John 10:10 we are told that "the thief" comes to kill, steal and destroy, but that Jesus came that we might have and enjoy life.

Satan is the thief, and one of the things he seeks to steal is our joy. If he can steal our joy from us, we will be weak, and when we are weak, the enemy takes advantage of us. Weak believers are no threat to him and his work of destruction.

In order to live as God intends for us to live, the first thing we must do is truly believe that it is God's will for us to experience continual joy. Then we must decide to enter into that joy. Below is a list of Scripture passages in which Jesus Himself revealed that it is God's will for us to enjoy life.

> **The thief comes only in order to steal and kill and destroy. I came that they may have and enjoy life, and have it in abundance (to the full, till it overflows).**
> **John 10:10**

> **I have told you these things, that My joy and delight may be in you, and that your joy and gladness may be of full measure and complete and overflowing.**
> **John 15:11**

> Up to this time you have not asked a [single] thing in My Name [as presenting all that I AM]; but now ask and keep on asking and you will receive, so that your joy (gladness, delight) may be full and complete.
>
> John 16:24

> And now I am coming to You [Father]; I say these things while I am still in the world, so that My joy may be made full and complete and perfect in them [the disciples] [that they may experience My delight fulfilled in them, that My enjoyment may be perfected in their own souls, that they may have My gladness within them, filling their hearts].
>
> John 17:13

Jesus wants us to experience enjoyment in our souls. It is important to our physical, mental, emotional and spiritual health. Proverbs 17:22 says, **A happy heart is good medicine and a cheerful mind works healing, but a broken spirit dries up the bones.**

It is God's will for us to enjoy life!

Now it is time to decide to enter into the full and abundant life that God wills for us. Joy and enjoyment are available, just as misery is available. Righteousness and peace are available, and so are condemnation and turmoil. There are blessings and curses available, and that is why Deuteronomy 30:19 tells us to choose, and to choose life and blessings.

There are many blessings available to God's children of which they never partake. The Promised Land was always available, and yet the Israelites wandered around in the wilderness forty years. Deuteronomy 1:2 states that the geographical distance of their journey was actually an eleven-day trip.

They were all around the Promised Land, close to it, even at the border, but refused to go in. They sent in spies to see if it was really as good as it sounded, but they did not enter. And the Bible tells us the reason they did not enter was unbelief. (Heb. 4:6 KJV.)

They simply would not believe what God told them. Therefore, they disobeyed Him. They walked in their own way, and their willful disobedience stole their joy. They wandered around in the wilderness murmuring, complaining, discouraged, fearful, impatient, filled with self-pity, blaming God and Moses for their situation.

Just think of how close they were all those forty years to the good life God had promised, but they refused to enter in. We must enter in, but to do so requires a daily decision — a strong, quality decision — not a weak, half-hearted, "we'll see what happens" decision.

There are different qualities and strengths of decisions, and any person who desires to live in the joy that Jesus said we could have will need to understand that he must be determined and ready to watch for all the *thieves of joy*. Also, he must be willing to make some radical changes in his approach to life's situations, as well as his lifestyle.

If you are hungry for true joy and enjoyment, if you are ready to learn to enjoy everything — even the seemingly mundane — then read on. If you are ready to enjoy the trip, open your heart to God and ask Him to show you all the things that are stealing your enjoyment.

As we continue, I will be sharing insight into many of the things that God has shown me to be thieves of joy in my own life. Some of them will speak to you, I am sure. Others may not fit your personal situation as well as they did mine, but the principles can be applied anywhere you need them.

This essay by Robert J. Hasting was given to me years ago, and I believe it expresses the point very well.

The Station

"Tucked away in our subconscious is an idyllic vision. We see ourselves on a long trip that spans the continent. We are traveling by train.

"Out the windows we drink in the passing scene of cars on nearby highways, of children waving at a crossing, of cattle grazing on a distant hillside, of smoke pouring from a power plant, of row upon row of corn and wheat, of flatlands and valleys, of mountains and rolling hillsides, of city skylines and village halls.

"But uppermost in our minds is the final destination. Bands will be playing and flags waving. Once we get there our dreams will come true, and the pieces of our lives will fit together like a jigsaw puzzle.

"How restlessly we pace the aisles...waiting, waiting, waiting for the station.

"'When we reach the station, that will be it,'" we cry.

"'When I'm 18...'

"'When I buy a new 450SL Mercedes-Benz...'

"'When I put the last kid through college...'

"'When I have paid off the mortgage...'

"'When I get a promotion...'

"'When I reach the age of retirement, I shall live happily ever after.'

"Sooner or later we must realize there is no station, no one place to arrive at once and for all. *The true joy of life is the trip* [emphasis mine]. The station is only a dream. It constantly outdistances us.

"'Relish the moment' is a good motto, especially when coupled with Psalm 118:24 (KJV), **This is the day which the Lord hath made; we will rejoice and be glad in it.**

"It isn't the burdens of today that drive men mad. It is the regrets over yesterday and the fear of tomorrow. Regret and fear are twin thieves who rob us of today.

"So stop pacing the aisles and counting the miles. Instead, climb more mountains, eat more ice cream, go barefoot more often, swim more rivers, watch more sunsets, laugh more, cry less.

"Life must be lived as we go along. The station will come soon enough."[3]

---

[3]Reprinted, by permission, from *The Station and Other Gems of Joy*, copyright © 1993 Robert J. Hastings.

3

Regret and Dread

I do not consider, brethren, that I have captured and made it my own [yet]; but one thing I do [it is my one aspiration]: forgetting what lies behind and straining forward to what lies ahead,

I press on toward the goal to win the [supreme and heavenly] prize to which God in Christ Jesus is calling us upward.

Philippians 3:13,14

Regret of the past and dread of the future are both "thieves of joy."

Let's examine each of them in detail to learn what causes them and how to avoid them as we continue our quest to enjoy the abundant life that God has provided for us through His Son Jesus.

Regret

Many people stay trapped in the past. There is only one thing that can be done about the past, and that is forget it.

When we make mistakes, as we all do, the only thing we can do is ask God's forgiveness and go on. Like Paul, we are all pressing toward the mark of perfection, but none of us has arrived.

I believe Paul enjoyed his life and ministry and this "one aspiration" of his was part of the reason why. Like us, he was pressing toward the mark of perfection, admitting that he had not arrived, but having insight on how to enjoy his life while he was making the trip.

That is a lesson we all must learn, as I can attest from personal experience. Let me illustrate.

My husband has always enjoyed sports, and I have never enjoyed them. He loves to watch ball games on television when he is home, which I used to hate because I felt it left me with nothing to do. So I would choose to "work." After all, if someone is enjoying his life, and you're not, a fleshly response can be to "work" in front of him while he is having a good time. Maybe it will make him feel guilty!

At least that is the way our carnal mind operates.

Our family had been to church one Sunday morning, and I was wondering what Dave had planned for the afternoon. I already had a bad attitude in my heart before I even asked the question because the NBA playoffs had been on television for two weeks, and he had been watching the games every night.

A bad attitude usually comes across in voice tone and body language. I asked the question, already angry about the answer I knew was coming. I certainly did not give God a chance to get involved because I already had a day of disaster mapped out in my mind.

We would go home and I would fix lunch, clean up the mess while the kids played, and Dave would watch another basketball game. Then I would clean the house (because all I ever do is work)!

While I was thinking about all this as we drove down the road, my daughter asked, "Daddy, are we going to get that new baseball channel on the cable network so we can watch baseball all the time?"

"I don't know," Dave responded, "I haven't made up my mind yet. I need to find out what it costs." And then he said, "Maybe we'll get rid of the Disney Channel and get the baseball channel instead. I never see anyone watching the Disney Channel anyway."

Immediately I chimed in with, "Danny watches the Disney Channel all the time, and you are not going to get rid of that for another baseball channel!"

Dave said something that I quickly responded to, then he said something else, and I said something back. Our voices got louder and louder until we were yelling at each other. By the time we got home, we were both angry, and the kids were upset because we were upset.

I waited for two hours for Dave to apologize to me, and he was not showing any signs of repentance. I fixed lunch, slamming bowls onto the table, making all the noise I could, and hoping to show my displeasure by my obvious upset. When the family came to the table to eat, I said I wasn't hungry and went to another room in the house. After they had finished eating, I cleaned the kitchen, then I proceeded to noisily clean the rest of the house.

I was already in ministry at the time, and I was scheduled to teach Bible college classes the next day at our church. I needed to prepare for my lesson, and it is impossible for me to study the Bible if I do not have total peace in my heart. I cannot approach God properly while I am angry at anyone. I knew that I needed to get beyond where I was emotionally, and it had become obvious that Dave was not feeling inclined to make the first move.

Finally, after telling God several times that I thought He should make Dave come and apologize to me, I reluctantly said, "All right! I'll go and apologize to him."

I went out where Dave was watching the ball game in the family room. The first time I walked by him, I just could not bring myself to say, "I'm sorry," so I went to the kitchen and then tried again to come back through. I was hoping to get something out of my mouth this time, but failed again.

I was so angry and so full of stubbornness that I felt I was about to explode. Yet God was dealing with me to make peace with my husband. I thought maybe I would exercise a while. I got out a piece of exercise equipment called a rebounder (a sort of mini-trampoline) and began to jump on it in the kitchen, thinking, "Well, maybe Dave will hear me out here and come out and apologize."

I had the rebounder sitting in the corner and had turned my face to the wall because I did not want to look at anyone who might come through the kitchen. My son Daniel, who was four years old at the time, came in and asked, "Mommy, why are you hiding from us?"

"I'm not hiding," I answered.

"Yes you are!" he replied. "You're jogging with your face in the corner."

That remark made me realize that I needed to grow up and stop acting like a baby. I knew I needed to get out of the corner and quit pouting. I went to Dave, and even though I still couldn't seem to say anything, I did bend over and kiss him.

"I love you," he said.

"I love you too," I answered, "but I would like to knock your head off," to which he replied, "I know, but you'll get over it."

We laughed, I went to the kitchen, ate my lunch and then went on to study.

What can be done about a situation like this once it has occurred? *Nothing!* The only thing to do is forget it and go on. Of course, I asked God to forgive me, but even after we ask for His forgiveness, we still have to choose to accept it and forgive ourselves, forget what has happened and go on with our lives.

24

I had already wasted about half my day by choosing to have a fleshly reaction to a family disagreement. Now the question was, what would I do with the rest of my day?

Until we learn to forget our mistakes and refuse to live in regret of the past, we will never really enjoy life.

Mistakes are a regular part of life, and I spent many years hating myself for each of my failures. I desperately wanted to be a good Christian. I wanted to please God. But I still thought it was my perfect performance that would please Him. I had not yet learned that He was pleased with my faith.

In Hebrews 11:6 we read, **But without faith it is impossible to please and be satisfactory to Him....**

Even when we make mistakes and waste precious time as a result of those mistakes, being upset when we could be enjoying life, it is useless to continue being miserable for an extended period of time because of the original mistake. Two wrongs never make anything right.

I had already wasted part of my day, I had apologized, and all was well, but I had to resist the temptation to spend the second half of my day regretting the first half.

If you made a mistake twenty years ago or ten minutes ago, there is still nothing you can do about it except ask for forgiveness, receive it, forget the past and go on. There may be some restitution you can make to the individual you hurt, and, if that is the case, by all means do so. But the "bottom line" is that you still must let go of the past in order to grasp the future. Until you do so, you will not enjoy life the way God intended when He sent Jesus.

Always remember that regret steals *now*!

God has called us to a faith walk. Faith operates in the *now* — at this time.

I believe that God has taken care of my past and my future, therefore, I do not have to live in regret or dread.

Hebrews 11:1 states, **Now faith is the assurance (the confirmation, the title deed) of the things [we] hope for, being the proof of things [we] do not see and the conviction of their reality [faith perceiving as real fact what is not revealed to the senses].**

This Scripture begins with the word "now." Although I know that the Greek word from which it is translated actually means "but, and, etc.,"[1] rather than "at this point in time," I still believe the term can be used to describe faith itself.

Faith operates *now*!

Without faith, I cannot enjoy my life. Every time I lay aside my faith and stop believing, I lose my peace, and as soon as I lose my peace, my joy goes with it.

There are many things we may find ourselves regretting.

One morning Dave woke me up at the usual time, and I had not had as much sleep as I needed so I decided to sleep a little while longer. I normally get up by 6:00 A.M., but this particular morning I said, "Let me sleep another forty-five minutes."

When Dave woke me up forty-five minutes later, the first thing I felt and thought was regret that I had not gotten up earlier.

You must understand that this is the way the devil works. God will tell you what you are about to do wrong, so you can change your mind before you make a mistake.

---

[1]James Strong, *The New Strong's Exhaustive Concordance of the Bible* (Nashville: Thomas Nelson Publishers, 1990), "Greek Dictionary of the New Testament," p. 21, entry #1161.

Satan waits until it's too late, when you can no longer do anything about it, and then tries to bring regret and ultimate condemnation upon you.

If it was going to be wrong for me to sleep an additional forty-five minutes, God would have, by His Spirit, made that point clear in my heart before I went back to sleep. He would not have waited until there was nothing I could do about it, and then fill me full of regret so I could not enjoy the rest of my day.

Even if you should oversleep, or go back to bed when in fact you should have been up early, regretting that situation is still not the answer. Repent, ask God to help you use more discipline and self-control the next time and then go on. If you have already wasted part of your day, getting sleep you did not actually need, there is no point in wasting more of it, regretting the part you have already wasted.

Have you ever eaten a meal at a restaurant and then spent the next few hours regretting that you had even gone there? Maybe the food did not really taste good to you, or perhaps you got poor service. You may have lost a lot of time or the atmosphere may not have been very nice. In any case, once the food was in your stomach, it didn't do any good to regret that you had spent your money on it.

This is one lesson I had to learn for myself because I am particular about what I eat. When I sit down to a meal, I like things a certain way. I like my coffee fresh, my food hot, my salads crisp, etc. Traveling as we do places Dave and me in many restaurants that we hope and pray are good, but we never know for sure until it's too late to change our minds.

I have had to learn to say, "Oh, well, it's only one meal out of many meals I will eat in my lifetime. I wish it had been better, but I'm not going to spend my time regretting that I went there."

You will find many areas in your own life in which Satan tries to cause you regret, which is one of the thieves of joy. Don't let him use regret to steal your enjoyment any longer.

Dread

Dread does the same thing to us that regret does, except that dread places us in the future, whereas regret puts us in the past.

I spent a lot of years with regret pulling on one arm and dread pulling on the other. The result was that I felt like I was being pulled apart, and I didn't even know what the problem was.

That is one of the reasons it makes me so happy to be able to share these truths with you, because I believe you can learn from my mistakes and avoid a lot of the misery I endured. Regret and dread are ruining the lives of multiplied thousands of people by stealing their joy and their enjoyment.

Perhaps when you began reading this book you were unhappy, discontented and lacking joy, and you had no idea why. I pray that your eyes are being opened.

I believe that sharing truth is one of the ways that Jesus opens blind eyes. Sometimes the blind eyes He opens are not physically blind eyes, but spiritually blind eyes.

Sometimes we think we need a miracle in our situation when what we truly need is a miracle of revelation that will change our attitude and alter our approach to life.

Dreading things can be a habit, an attitude that develops out of lethargy or laziness. Procrastination and dread often work together. An upcoming task is dreaded, so procrastination says, "Put it off until later." That sounds good for a few minutes, but the thing is still there to be dreaded until it is finished. It would be far better to do it and be free to go on to other things.

Our youngest son, Daniel, had a habit of putting things off, especially in the area of work. He did not procrastinate on fun, but he did on work. God literally spoke to his heart, and it brought revelation to his life. The Holy Spirit said to him, "It takes more effort and energy to try to get out of work than it does to go ahead and do it."

You may not know it, but dread is a close relative of fear.

We know that God has not given us a spirit of fear (2 Tim. 1:7 KJV), and since He did not give us fear, we know that He did not give us dread either. As a matter of fact, the Bible teaches us in several places not to dread.

In Deuteronomy 1:29,30 we read the words of Moses spoken to the Children of Israel about their enemies who held possession of the Promised Land: **Then I said to you, Dread not, neither be afraid of them. The Lord your God Who goes before you, He will fight for you just as He did for you in Egypt before your eyes.**

Notice that verse 30 speaks of "the Lord Who goes before you." Jesus is our Pioneer. (Heb. 2:10.) That means that He goes out ahead of us and makes a way for us. When a project seems impossible or unpleasant, trust your Pioneer (Jesus) to go ahead of you and pave the way.

Perhaps you are going to have to be with people you feel do not accept you. You don't enjoy being around them because they make you feel rejected. Instead of dreading the event as you normally would, spend the same spiritual energy trusting your Pioneer to go ahead of you and make the way easy.

Dread is like fear — it draws disaster. It is Satan's open door to bring in the thing feared or dreaded.

I have found that dreading a task is actually more painful than doing it. Once I do it, it is finished, but as long as I put off doing it, the dread lingers on and on.

First Chronicles 22:13 is another Scripture that warns against dread. In this verse King David spoke to the Israelites and told them, **Then you will prosper if you are careful to keep and fulfill the statutes and ordinances with which the Lord charged Moses concerning Israel. Be strong and of good courage. Dread not and fear not; be not dismayed.**

It seems to me that this Scripture is saying that dread and fear will not only keep us from fulfilling God's Word, but, as a result, it will also hinder our prosperity.

According to Hebrews 11:6, rewards come to those who believe that God exists and who diligently seek Him — those who operate in faith. In Romans 14:23, Paul says that whatever is not of faith is sin. I believe we can say with assurance that dread is not faith.

That which is dreaded may be something major or even something minor. Some people dread getting up in the morning, driving to work, fighting the traffic, facing confrontation, handling the boss or their employees, coming back home after work. They dread washing the dishes, going to the grocery store, doing the laundry, cleaning out the closet, dealing with family members and issues, even going to bed at night.

In your own life, you may want some new clothes, but dread going shopping. Perhaps you would like to see a friend or relative who lives some distance away, but you don't want to go because you dread the drive. The trip could be made pleasant by a change of attitude. Use the time wisely by praying or listening to tapes.

Most people dread exercise, but it is something we all need. It is important for me to get some kind of aerobic exercise, so I walk on a treadmill. Like most people, I find myself wanting the benefits of exercise, and yet negative thoughts fill my mind and feelings of dread pour over my emotions. I do not have to keep them just because the devil offers them to me. I have learned to say no! As soon as the Holy Spirit makes me aware of the presence of dread, I say, "No, I'm not going to dread it — I'm just going to do it."

If I let *dread* prevent me from doing my exercise, then I will *regret* that I did not do it. I use the time I spend on the exercise machine in prayer. Sometimes I have my secretary sit with me and we do office business while I exercise.

When exercising, it is possible to listen to music or tapes or even watch television. An adjustment in attitude and approach can change everything.

Let this be a day of decision for you — a day when you decide to no longer operate in regret and dread. Become a *now* person. Live in the present, not the past or the future. God has a plan for your life now. Trust Him today. Don't put it off another day.

Believing God brings you into His rest and puts an end to the torment caused by living in regret and dread, but you must take action to believe God today. Don't wait until tomorrow.

The writer of Hebrews 4:7 said of the Lord, **Again He sets a definite day, [a new] Today, [and gives another opportunity of securing that rest] saying through David after so long a time in the words already quoted, Today, if you would hear His voice and when you hear it, do not harden your hearts.**

I believe this word applies to everyone who is reading it right now! As you hear the Word of God, as you hear His voice, do not harden your heart. Believe today and begin today to refuse to live in regret and dread. Let this book be your point of contact to release your faith and take hold of God's promise to take care of your past and your future.

In Hebrews 4:2 we are told that the Israelites heard this same message but it did not benefit them because they did not mix faith with it. I have learned that we can hear and hear about the promises of God, but the time comes when we must release our faith and say, "That is mine, and I will not live one more day without doing everything I can to enjoy it."

Take the Pressure Off

I have learned from experience that living life one day at a time is something that can be done.

God gives me grace for today, but He does not give me grace today for yesterday or tomorrow. When I am trying to live yesterday today, it brings great pressure. The same thing happens if I am out into the future, dreading it or trying to figure it out. I have even discovered that it will make me grouchy, because I have to do it under pressure.

When God anoints something, there is a Holy Spirit ease to it. Oil is one of the symbols of the Holy Spirit, and oil speaks of ease. When that oil or anointing is not there, everything becomes hard.

Without the anointing, things have to be done under pressure. Living in regret and dread is pressure.

Take the pressure off, believe God and enter His rest.

Be a *now* person.

4

Joy and Peace Are Found in Believing

For the kingdom of God is not meat and drink; but righteousness, and peace, and joy in the Holy Ghost.
Romans 14:17 KJV

Joy is never released through unbelief, but it is always present where there is belief.

Believing is so much simpler than not believing.

If we do not believe God, His Word and promises, then we are left with the labor of reasoning and attempting to work out matters ourselves.

The writer of Hebrews 4:3 noted that we who have believed enter the rest of God. In Hebrews 4:10 he wrote: **For he who has once entered [God's] rest also has ceased from [the weariness and pain] of human labors....**

In Matthew 11:28 Jesus said: **Come to Me, all you who labor and are heavy-laden and overburdened, and I will cause you to rest. [I will ease and relieve and refresh your souls.]**

Jesus instructed us to come to Him, but *how* are we to come to Him? In Hebrews 11:6 we read: **But without faith it is impossible to please and be satisfactory to Him. For whoever would come near to God must [necessarily] believe that God exists and that He is the rewarder of those who earnestly and diligently seek Him [out].** That means that when we come to God, we must do so believing. When we do, we will have joy, and where there is joy, there will also be enjoyment.

"What's the Matter With Me?"

One night I seemed to be very miserable. I was just walking around my house doing what I needed to do, but not happy, not enjoying life.

"What's the matter with me, Lord?" I asked. "What is my problem?"

It seemed that something was lurking within me, something that kept draining the joy out of me. As I wandered around the house, I began looking at a Scripture box I kept on my desk.

I flipped it open and the Holy Spirit within me instantly confirmed the Scripture that came up: **May the God of your hope so fill you with all joy and peace in believing [through the experience of your faith] that by the power of the Holy Spirit you may abound and be overflowing (bubbling over) with hope** (Rom. 15:13).

I knew immediately that a large part of my problem was simply that I was doubting instead of believing. I was doubting the call of God on my life, wondering if He would meet our financial need, questioning my decisions and actions, etc.

I had become negative instead of positive.

I was doubting instead of believing.

Doubt is an attitude that can easily creep up on us; that's why we must be watchful not to permit it to do so.

Doubt certainly may knock at the door of your heart. When it does, answer with a believing heart, and you will always maintain the victory.

The doubtful, negative mind is filled with reasoning. It rotates around and around the circumstance or situation, attempting to find answers for it. In the Word of God we are not instructed to search for our own answers. We are, however, instructed to trust God with all of our heart and mind. (Prov. 3:5.) When we follow the guidelines the Lord has laid out for us, they will unerringly bring us to joy and peace.

Joy Defined

This is God's will for us, that we might have and enjoy life. Jesus did not die for you and me that we might be miserable. He died to deliver us from every kind of oppression and misery. His work is already finished, and the only thing that remains to be accomplished is for us to *believe.*

My understanding of joy, resulting from years of studying the subject, is that it covers a wide range of emotions, from calm delight to extreme hilarity. The times of extreme hilarity are fun, and we all need those moments of laughing and laughing until our sides hurt. We probably won't live our lives that way on a day-to-day basis, but we need those times. Later in the book I will discuss the value of laughter. God has given us an ability to laugh, so there must be a reason!

We should grow in our ability to enjoy life and be able to say, "I live my life in a state of calm delight." I think calm delight is a mixture of peace and joy.

According to *Vine's Complete Expository Dictionary of Old and New Testament Words,* some of the Greek words relating to joy in the Bible mean "delight," "gladness," "exceeding joyful," "exuberant joy," "to exult, rejoice greatly...with exceeding joy."[1] An explanatory note in Vine's biblical dictionary says, "'Joy' is associated with life...."[2]

---

[1]W.E. Vine, Merrill Unger, and William White, Jr., *Vine's Complete Expository Dictionary of Old and New Testament Words* (Nashville: Thomas Nelson, Inc., 1985), pp. 335-336.
[2]Vine, p. 336.

Webster defines the word *joy* as "great pleasure or happiness: DELIGHT," "The expression or display of this emotion," "A source or object of pleasure or satisfaction," and (in the archaic form) "To fill with joy," or "To enjoy."[3]

In Vine's biblical dictionary, the two Greek words translated *enjoy* in the King James Bible are 1) *tunchano*, a verb meaning "to reach, get, obtain," which is also translated "enjoy (i.e., obtain to our satisfaction)" and, 2) *apolausis*, a noun meaning "enjoyment," which is a form of another Hebrew word *apolauo* meaning "to take hold of, enjoy a thing," and "suggests the advantage or pleasure to be obtained from a thing."[4]

In Webster's dictionary, the verb *enjoy* is defined as "to rejoice," "to derive pleasure from: RELISH," "to have the benefit or use of" (as in the expression "enjoys good living") and "to make happy" (as in the phrase "enjoying themselves with a new game").[5]

Have and Enjoy Life

In John 10:10 we see that Jesus came so we might have and enjoy life. They are two different things to me. It is possible to be alive and not enjoy life.

Webster used the word "relish" to define enjoyment. Think about it like this: People put relish on hot dogs or sandwiches to make them taste better. These foods can be eaten without the relish, but the relish adds to the flavor, the enjoyment, of them.

Life is the same way. We can blandly live our lives, going through the motions of working, accomplishing, doing — and never truly enjoying life.

---

[3]*Webster's II New College Dictionary*, s.v. "joy."

[4]Vine, p. 201.

[5]*Webster's II New Riverside University Dictionary*, s.v. "enjoy."

Enjoying life is a decision, just like putting relish on a hot dog is a decision. Jesus gave us life so we can derive pleasure from being alive, not just so we can go through the motions and try to survive until He comes back for us or takes us home.

Life should be celebrated!

Celebrate Life

But the fruit of the [Holy] Spirit [the work which His presence within accomplishes] is love, *joy (gladness)*, peace, patience (an even temper, forbearance), kindness, goodness (benevolence), faithfulness,

Gentleness (meekness, humility), self-control (self-restraint, continence)....

Galatians 5:22,23

Doubt and unbelief are thieves of joy, but simple childlike believing releases the joy that is resident in our spirits because of the Holy Spirit Who lives in us. As we see in Galatians 5:22,23, one of the fruits of the Holy Spirit is joy. Therefore, since we are filled with God's Holy Spirit, we believers should express joy and enjoy our lives.

We might look at it like this, joy is in the deepest part of the person who has accepted Jesus as his Savior — joy is in his spirit. But if his soul (his mind, will and emotions) is filled with worry, negative thoughts, reasoning, doubt and unbelief, these negative things will become like a wall that holds back the release of the fruit of joy resident in him.

The Apostle Peter said to cast all our care (anxieties, worries, concerns) on the Lord. (1 Pet. 5:7.) Paul exhorted the believers of his day, **Be anxious for nothing, but in everything by prayer and supplication,** *with thanksgiving,* **let your requests be made known to God; and the** *peace* **of God, which surpasses all understanding, will guard your** *hearts* **and** *minds* **through Christ Jesus** (Phil. 4:6,7 NKJV).

Keep your mind filled with happy, glad thoughts, and, as you trust God, He will take care of your problems.

Believe!

Jesus replied, This is the work (service) that God asks of you: that you believe....

John 6:29

God's plan for us is actually so simple that many times we miss it. We tend to look for something more complicated — something more difficult — that we are expected to do to please God. Jesus has told us what we are to do to please the Father, "Believe!"

Jesus also said, **Truly I say to you, whoever does not accept and receive and welcome the kingdom of God like a little child [does] shall not in any way enter it [at all]** (Luke 18:17).

A few years ago, I began to realize that I was a very complicated person and that my habit of complicating things was stealing my joy — it was preventing me from really enjoying life. It was then that God began to speak to me about simplicity.

Frequently, I write in a journal or notebook the things that God is teaching me or dealing with me about. Here are some of the things I wrote in October 1988:

"I have been struggling inwardly for a long time with something I cannot even define. I think God is bringing me up out of being complicated and trying to teach me to 'be,' instead of 'do' all the time. He is trying to teach me to enjoy simple things.

"It seems I keep looking for something to do in my free time that I will really enjoy and I keep coming up with nothing. Tonight, it seems the Lord said to me, 'Learn to enjoy the simple things in life.' And then I wrote, 'God help me. I'm not even sure I know what simplicity is.'"

I have had to learn and am still learning what simplicity is and how to approach things with a simple attitude. One of the things I have learned is that *believing is much simpler than doubting*. Doubt brings in confusion and often depression. It causes us to speak doubtful and negative things out of our mouths.

Believing, on the other hand, releases joy and leaves us free to enjoy life while God is taking care of our circumstances and situations. It sounds almost too good to be true, and that is exactly why many people never enter into God's plan. There are countless thousands upon thousands of people who have accepted Jesus as their Savior. They are on their way to heaven, but they are not enjoying the trip.

It is like a person who was given a brand new home as a gift. He is presented with the keys — to the garage, the front door, the back door, the basement door and all the rooms in the house that have locks on them. The home belongs to him, but he can own it all his life and never live in it and enjoy it if he does not use the keys to open the doors and enter in.

Often the thing that keeps us from entering into and enjoying the life that God has freely bestowed upon us is our own sin consciousness.

Sin

For we have not an high priest which cannot be touched with the feeling of our infirmities; but was in all points tempted like as we are, yet without sin.

Let us therefore come boldly unto the throne of grace, that we may obtain mercy, and find grace to help in time of need.

Hebrews 4:15,16 KJV

Let's examine the subject of sin. People struggle with their sins, and often it is one of the chief causes of their not entering into the joy-filled life Jesus died to give them.

Sin is a real problem for most people, and the interesting thing is, sin does not have to be a big problem.

Do you know that God has already made provision in His Word for human mistakes, weaknesses and failures? Most people make a much bigger deal out of these things than God does in His Word.

Hebrews 4:15,16 tells us that *Jesus understands* our human frailty because He was tempted in every way that we are, yet without sinning. Therefore, because He is our High Priest, interceding with the Father for us, we can come boldly to God's throne to receive the grace, favor, mercy and help that we need.

Believe and Receive

Notice that the Scripture says that we come to the throne of God to *receive*. I want to emphasize this point because in a sense the word "receive" is synonymous with the word "believe."

Webster's dictionary says that to *believe* means "to accept as true or real."[6] The same dictionary says that to *receive* means to "take something (something given, offered, or transmitted)."[7]

In the spiritual realm, when you and I believe something, we receive it into our heart. If a physical manifestation is needed, it will come after we have believed — not before. In the world, we are taught to believe what we see. In God's Kingdom, we must learn to believe first and then we will see manifested what we have believed (received, admitted in our heart).

In Mark 11:23,24 Jesus told His disciples, **Truly I tell you, whoever says to this mountain, Be lifted up and**

---

[6]*Webster's II New Riverside University Dictionary,* s.v. "believe."

[7]*Webster's II New Riverside University Dictionary,* s.v. "receive."

thrown into the sea! and does not doubt at all in his heart but *believes* that what he says will take place, it will be done for him. For this reason I am telling you, whatever you ask for in prayer, *believe* (trust and be confident) that it is granted to you, and *you will [get it]*.

When Jesus said that whatever we ask of God, believing, will be *granted* to us, He was saying that we will receive it *free*.

One of our biggest challenges is that we do not trust the word "free." We quickly find out in the world's system that things really are not free. Even when we are told they are free, there is usually a hidden cost somewhere.

But, in God's economy, things are different. Everything comes to us as a gift, and the only thing one can do with a gift is receive it graciously with a thankful heart. Salvation and continual forgiveness of our sins are gifts bestowed upon us by God because of our acceptance of His Son Jesus Christ.

When we make a mistake, display a weakness or fail in any way, we can doubt that God loves us, wonder if He is angry at us, try to do all kinds of good works to atone for our failure and give up our joy as a sacrifice for our error. Or, we can simply *believe* what we read in 1 John 1:9, **If we [freely] admit that we have sinned and confess our sins, He [God] is faithful and just (true to His own nature and promises) and will forgive our sins [dismiss our lawlessness] and [continuously] cleanse us from all unrighteousness [everything not in conformity to His will in purpose, thought, and action].**

I am personally also very partial to the words of John as recorded in 1 John 2:1,2, **My little children, I write you these things so that you may not violate God's law and sin. But if anyone should sin, we have an Advocate (One Who will intercede for us) with the Father — [it is] Jesus Christ [the all] righteous [upright, just, Who conforms to** the Father's will in every purpose, thought, and action]. And He [that same Jesus Himself] is the propitiation (the atoning sacrifice) for our sins, and not for ours alone but also for [the sins of] the whole world.

Here John was saying, "Do your best not to sin, but when you do make a mistake, Jesus is interceding for you and has already paid for your error."

In our conferences, I tell people who make a decision to believe in Jesus as their Savior, "Jesus has forgiven every sin — not only the wrong things you have done, but every wrong thing you ever will do. He has already paid for your sins and errors and has determined to cleanse you from them."

No wonder the Gospel is called "good news." But remember, all these wonderful blessings, freedoms and gifts are received through believing.

Luke chapter two records that after the birth of Jesus, an angel appeared to shepherds tending their flocks in the field: **...the angel said to them, Do not be afraid; for behold, I bring you good news of a** *great joy* **which will come to all the people. For to you is born this day in the town of David a Savior, Who is Christ (the Messiah) the Lord!** (Luke 2:10,11).

We can see from this one Scripture that when properly understood, believed and received, the Gospel is supposed to bring great joy — not condemnation for sin.

I don't spend my time meditating on my sins. There was a time in my life when, if you had asked me, "What was the last thing you did wrong, Joyce?" I could have told you exactly what I had last done wrong, the precise time I had done it and how long I had been paying for it.

I was *sin* conscious! Now I am *righteousness* conscious! I *believe* I have been made the righteousness of God in Christ. (2 Cor. 5:21.)

If you asked me the same question now, I would really have to stop and think about it. It's not that I no longer do anything wrong, but I do take care of my sins scripturally, letting go of what lies behind and pressing on to what lies ahead. (Phil. 3:13,14.)

God has delivered me from self-analysis and self-preservation. By that I mean that I no longer worry about every tiny error I make, and I no longer deceive myself into thinking that I can "keep myself from sin."

Instead, when I fail, as we all do, I remind myself that the Lord is my keeper, and that it is He Who will keep me from all evil, as we read in Psalm 121:3-5,7,8: **He will not allow your foot to slip or to be moved; He Who keeps you will not slumber. Behold, He who keeps Israel will neither slumber nor sleep. The Lord is your keeper; the Lord is your shade on your right hand [the side not carrying a shield]....The Lord will keep you from all evil; He will keep your life. The Lord will keep your going out and your coming in from this time forth and forevermore.**

Also consider Jude 24, **Now to Him Who is able to keep you without stumbling or slipping or falling, and to present [you] unblemished (blameless and faultless) before the presence of His glory in triumphant joy and exultation [with unspeakable, ecstatic delight].**

If we release God's keeping power by believing Scriptures like the ones I have just quoted, the fruit of such belief will be triumphant joy and exultation with unspeakable, ecstatic delight. That sounds really good to me, how about you?

I lost my joy many times trying to keep myself from making mistakes, but once I learned to trust the Lord to keep me from falling, I no longer had to major in my failures. My behavior began to improve and is still doing so. The mistakes I make in the process are already forgiven.

43

All I need to do is admit my failures, confess them and *receive/believe* in the mercy of God to cleanse me from all unrighteousness.

Once I made that discovery, for the first time in my life I was able to truly begin enjoying the Lord.

Enjoy God

The high call on the life of every believer — the goal each of us should strive for — is to enjoy God. According to John 1:4 and John 14:6, He is Life, and my conclusion was that I could not enjoy God unless I learned to enjoy life.

None of us can enjoy God if we are concerned that He is angry with us most of the time due to our sins.

Jesus came to deliver us from the wrong kind of fear in our relationship with our heavenly Father. We should be relaxed in His presence. We need to have reverential fear, the kind that provokes respect, honor and obedience. But we must cleanse our hearts and minds of any thoughts that the Lord is angry with us. According to His Word, He is full of mercy and compassion, and is slow to anger. (Neh. 9:17.)

A few years ago, the Lord said to me, "Joyce, I am not nearly as hard to get along with as most of you think I am." We are no surprise to God. He knew what He was getting when He drew us into relationship with Himself.

Psalm 139 states that before He formed us in the womb, God knew us! He already knows the things you and I will do wrong in the future that we have no idea about now. It is not our sin that stops us — it is unbelief!

God has made ample provision for our failures, but our greatest failure, He can do nothing about. Why? Because our greatest failure is the failure to believe what He said. To believe is our part. He does all the rest, but it is our decision to choose life or death, believing or doubting, joy or misery.

The Deeper Life

We live too much on the surface.

In Luke 5:4 Jesus instructed Simon Peter and the other fishermen in the boat with him, **...Put out into the deep...,and lower your nets for a haul.**

Do you want a haul of blessings in your life? If the answer is yes, and I am sure it is, then you have to leave the shallows of living according to what you think and feel and begin to live the deeper life according to what you know down deep inside.

Faith is deposited in the spirit. Romans 12:3 says that every man is given a measure of faith. Faith is a force that comes out of the spirit, and it will accomplish great things, but faith must have agreement.

I look at it this way. I may have the faith in my heart to step out and do something, but if I begin to counsel with my mind, negative, doubtful and unbelieving thoughts can talk me right out of what I know deep inside.

When I say that faith must have agreement, what I mean is that if I have faith in my heart but my head believes the opposite, I will not see what I believe come to pass.

The Ben Campbell Johnson interpretive paraphrase of Mark 11:22,23 gives some insight on this point: **Jesus said, "Trust in God. Truly, anyone who speaks to that mountain yonder saying, 'Dump yourself in the lake,' and does not become separated from the statement he makes — that person will actualize his statement...."**

The Amplified Bible translates Jesus' words in verse 23 as referring to anyone who believes and does not doubt. Mr. Johnson translates them as referring to anyone who does not become separated from his own statements. I really like that way of stating this principle because we often do just what this verse warns against. We believe one thing if we look deep inside our hearts, and we believe another if we listen to our minds.

We must understand that Satan is the thief. He comes only in order to kill, steal and destroy. Every blessing that Jesus has provided, Satan desires to steal. Righteousness, peace and joy are the top three on the list. According to Romans 14:17 KJV, the Kingdom of God is righteousness, peace and joy; be assured that Satan is out to steal the Kingdom. Believe what the Word of God says; exalt it above your own thoughts or feelings.

In 2 Corinthians 10:5 (KJV and AMP) the Apostle Paul wrote of casting down wrong imaginations and every high and lofty thing (or thought) that exalts itself against the true knowledge of God.

Frequently we hear the Word of God, and we believe it when we hear it. In Romans 10:17 KJV we read that **...faith cometh by hearing, and hearing by the word of God**. When the Word is heard, faith is imparted to believe it. But the question is, once we have heard the Word and believed it, do we continue to believe it?

Often, we leave the place where we have heard the Word and return to meditating on our circumstances, once again separating ourselves from what was planted in our hearts. The seed that was sown is stolen. You might say, the Word is eaten up by the fowl (Mark 4:4 KJV) — the foul spirits Satan sends out to attack the minds of those who hear. (Mark 4:15.)

Believers Are Supposed To Believe

As I close this chapter, I would like to encourage you to remember something that I think will help you when doubt comes: *Believers are called believers because they are supposed to believe!* It is just that simple, believe.

As a believer, your part is to believe. Stay positive, keep it simple and believe. ·

I tell people that they would be better off to believe and never see any results than not to believe and never see any results. (Believing will produce good results, but I am making a point.)

Believing keeps your heart full of joy. So at least, if you believe and never see results, you will be happy. If you do not believe, you will never see positive results in your life, and you will be miserable, in addition to poverty-stricken in every area of living.

If you make the decision that you definitely want to enjoy life more, then you must also decide to do something about the thieves of doubt and unbelief, because without a believing heart it is impossible to enjoy the journey of faith.

5

Simplicity

And Jesus answered and said to her, "Martha, Martha, you are worried and troubled about many things.

"But one thing is needed...."

Luke 10:41,42 NKJV

As I said in the previous chapter, I came to a place in life where I knew that God was dealing with me about simplicity. At the time, I was very complicated in most everything I did. I could not even entertain friends without complicating it.

Not only were my actions complicated but also my thought processes. I complicated my relationship with the Lord because I had a legalistic approach to righteousness. To me, life itself was complicated. I felt that I had a lot of complex problems, and I didn't realize they were that way only because my approach to life was complicated.

When we are complicated inside, then everything else in life seems that way to us.

Is Life Complicated or Simple?

Webster defines the word *complicate* as "to make or become complex, intricate, or bewildering," or "to twist or become twisted together."[1] According to this definition, if something is *complicated*, it is "difficult to understand."[2]

---

[1] *Webster's II New Riverside University Dictionary*, s.v. "complicate."

[2] *Webster's II New Riverside University Dictionary*, s.v. "complicated."

On the other hand, Webster defines *simple* as "having or composed of only one thing or part," "not complex: EASY," "without additions or modifications," "unassuming or unpretentious," "not deceitful: SINCERE," "having no divisions," "without overtones."[3]

We can learn a lot just from meditating on these definitions. For example: To *complicate* is "to twist together." We can see from that definition that if doubt and unbelief are mixed or twisted together with belief, the result will be complication.

One definition of *complicated* is "bewildering." When I mix doubt and unbelief with belief, I feel bewildered, not knowing what to do, but busily trying to figure it out. I hear so much of this same thing from people in the Body of Christ who talk with me or ask me for prayer. They are bewildered. Their problems seem to be too much for them. They wonder why their prayers are not heard or answered.

In James 1:6-8 we read that the double-minded (complicated, bewildered) man is unstable in all his ways and that he should not think that he will receive anything he asks from the Lord — and that includes wisdom and guidance.

Whereas something complicated is "complex, intricate and bewildering" and "difficult to understand," anything simple is easy to understand because it is "composed of only one thing."

For years I sought for many things — answers to my situations, prosperity, healing, success in my ministry, changes in my family, etc. Finally, I learned about the "one thing" I was supposed to be seeking.

Centuries ago the psalmist wrote, **One thing have I asked of the Lord, that will I seek, inquire for, and**

---

[3]*Webster's II New Riverside University Dictionary*, s.v. "simple."

[insistently] require: that I may dwell in the house of the Lord [in His presence] all the days of my life, to behold and gaze upon the beauty [the sweet attractiveness and the delightful loveliness] of the Lord and to meditate, consider, and inquire in His temple (Ps. 27:4).

I realized that I should have been seeking the "one thing" instead of the many things.

When we seek the Lord, He takes care of all the other things, as Jesus promised in Matthew 6:33: **But seek (aim at and strive after) first of all His [God's] kingdom and His righteousness (His way of doing and being right), and then all these things** [you desire and seek after] **taken together will be given you besides.**

The account of Mary and Martha also depicts this truth.

Many Things or One Thing?

Now while they were on their way, it occurred that Jesus entered a certain village, and a woman named Martha received and welcomed Him into her house.

And she had a sister named Mary, who seated herself at the Lord's feet and was listening to His teaching.

But Martha [overly occupied and too busy] was distracted with much serving; and she came up to Him and said, Lord, is it nothing to You that my sister has left me to serve alone? Tell her then to help me [to lend a hand and do her part along with me]!

But the Lord replied to her by saying, Martha, Martha, you are anxious and troubled about many things;

There is need of only one or but a few things. Mary has chosen the good portion [that which is to her advantage], which shall not be taken away from her.

Luke 10:38-42

Martha was worried and anxious about many things, but Mary was concerned about only one thing.

Martha was doing what I used to do, running around trying to make everything perfect in order to impress God and everyone else. In my former days, I was concerned about my reputation, about what people thought. I felt better about myself when I was working. I felt that I had worth as long as I was accomplishing something. Like Martha, I resented people like Mary who enjoyed themselves; I thought they should be doing what I was doing.

Now, obviously there is a time to work (John 5:17), and accomplishment is good. The Bible teaches us that we are to bear good, abundant fruit, and when we do, our Father in heaven is glorified. (John 15:8.) But, I was out of balance.

Martha certainly has her place, but so does Mary. My problem was that I was all Martha and no Mary. I loved Jesus, but I had not yet learned about the simple life He desired me to live.

Difficult or Easy?

One part of the definition of *simple* is "easy."

My life certainly was not easy. Nothing about me was.

It seemed to me that everything was easy for my husband, and nothing was easy for me. He enjoyed life, and I did not. He "cast his care upon the Lord" (1 Pet. 5:7), and I was **anxious and troubled about many things.** (Luke 10:41). He was calm, cool and collected, and I fretted and fumed all the time, living in a constant state of upset and worry.

There were times when I resented Dave because things seemed so easy for him and so difficult for me. He was free, and I was caught in a trap. I did not know how I got there, or how to get out.

I really did not realize at the time God began dealing with me about simplicity just how complicated I made things, nor was I able to just rebuke "the demon of complication" and go free. I had a lot to learn. I had a lot of bad habits to break, and there were a lot of new ones that needed to be formed in me. Most of them involved the way I approached situations.

It really wasn't that life was so complicated, it was my approach to life that was so complex.

When I started looking for Scriptures on the subject of simplicity, I found only a few, but here is one that I did discover. It was part of a letter written by Paul to the believers in Corinth: **But I fear, lest somehow, as the serpent deceived Eve by his craftiness, so your minds may be corrupted from the *simplicity* that is in Christ** (2 Cor. 11:3 NKJV).

The Old Covenant was complicated. It was filled with regulations — do's and don'ts. The Law was complicated in itself, but the complication was compounded by the fact that man was supposed to keep it perfectly, and he had no ability to do so. Not knowing that he was not able to do so, he continually struggled to do something that couldn't be done without a Savior.

If you want to live a complicated, complex, joyless life, spend your time trying to do something that can't be done!

Simplify Your Life!

The Apostle Paul had been given tremendous grace by Jesus and was commissioned to teach grace to the Jewish people. In 2 Corinthians 11:3, Paul was apparently concerned that even though some of the believers in Corinth had learned about the simple life, and were aware of the wonderful simplicity that was available to them through Jesus Christ, they were in danger of being deceived and losing that simplicity.

I would say to you that as you progress in simplifying your life, always remember to do as Paul instructed the church in Galatia: **In [this] freedom Christ has made us free [and completely liberated us]; stand fast then, and do not be hampered and held ensnared and submit again to a yoke of slavery [which you have once put off]** (Gal. 5:1).

If you are ever to live simply, you must be determined to gain your freedom and even more determined to keep it.

The second Scripture I found on simplicity is 2 Corinthians 1:12 KJV, and it connects simplicity and rejoicing: **For our rejoicing is this, the testimony of our conscience, that in simplicity and godly sincerity, not with fleshly wisdom, but by the grace of God, we have had our conversation in the world, and more abundantly to you-ward.** In this context, the word *conversation* means "conduct" or "behavior."[4]

Here Paul was saying, "We have joy because we have conducted ourselves in simplicity and godly sincerity, not with fleshly wisdom, which always includes a lot of reasoning, but we have lived by the grace of God."

Nothing is more simple than grace.[5]

Simplicity or Complexity?

I used to wonder why there aren't more Scriptures about simplicity, or why the Bible doesn't talk more about it, especially since it seems to be a much needed and sorely abused subject.

The Holy Spirit showed me that the entire New Covenant is simple. It may not frequently use the word "simple," but it is the essence of simplicity, as we see in God's plan of redemption for mankind:

---

[4]*Webster's Ninth New Collegiate Dictionary*, s.v. "conversation."

[5]If you have not read my book titled, *If Not For the Grace of God*, I recommend that you do so. See the book list in the back of this book.

Jesus came and paid for our sins, taking our punishment upon Himself. He became our substitute, paid the debt we owed, at no cost to us. He did all this freely because of His great love, grace and mercy.

He inherited all the Father has to give and tells us that we are joint-heirs with Him by virtue of our faith. He has provided the way for our complete victory both here and hereafter. We are more than conquerors. He has conquered, and we get the reward without the battle.

I could go on and on, but I am sure you get the point.

How much simpler could it be? It is not complicated. We complicate it!

Complication is the work of Satan. When we return to and maintain simplicity, we are warring against him. He hates simplicity, because he knows the power and the joy that it brings.

I also looked for books on simplicity and did not find many of them either. I had to be very open to the Holy Spirit to teach me as I went. Usually, personal experience is the best teacher anyway. I began to systematically watch for times when I had no joy and then asked myself why. Often, I discovered that it was because I was complicating an issue. Here is an example:

Dave and I had an argument one evening close to bedtime. Dave is an easy-going man who has no problem just forgetting things and going on. We said what we both felt that we needed to say, and as far as Dave was concerned it was over and time to go to bed. He lay down and went right to sleep, and I went into my home office to try to figure out what had happened.

How had we managed to get into an argument? And, what could I do to be sure it never happened again?

We must be realistic — not idealistic. Realism says plainly that two people probably will not live together the rest of their lives in complete and total agreement.

Idealism says, "I am going to do this perfectly."

Idealistic people usually do not enjoy life. They have perfect ideas about how things should be, and when they do not work out that way, they are disappointed.

I was determined that I would get myself an answer, and the longer I stayed up (supposedly seeking God), the more frustrated I became. Finally about one o'clock in the morning, I said, "Lord, what am I going to do?"

He answered and said, "Why not simply go to bed?"

Here is another example:

Entertaining friends and guests in our home was something I wanted to do, but never really enjoyed in the end. As I opened my heart to God, He began to show me that I made a project out of it. I could make plans for a simple barbecue with three couples besides Dave and me, and, before it was over, turn it into a nightmare.

Much complication is born out of an ungodly need to impress people.

I was abused in my childhood and, as a result, I was very insecure about myself. People who are insecure normally strive to impress others because they feel they are not very impressive just being who they are.

When I entertained, everything had to be perfect — just the right food and drinks, the house immaculate, the yard manicured and all the lawn furniture spotless. All the children had to look like they just stepped out of a fashion magazine, and, of course, I had to have on just the right outfit, and every single hair had to be in place.

I worked so hard outwardly and inwardly before the event started that I was worn out by the time our guests arrived. Even their arrival did not put an end to my labor. I continued to work most of the time they were there — setting food out and putting food away, washing dishes and sweeping the kitchen floor so none of the crumbs would get tracked onto my carpets.

Then I would have resentment in my heart and quite often in my mouth, because it seemed that everyone else had fun and enjoyed themselves, and all I did was work.

Finally, I had to face the truth that I was creating the problem. I could have taken a much simpler approach. I could have grilled some hot dogs and hamburgers, heated up some baked beans and set out a bowl of potato chips.

I didn't have to buy steaks that we couldn't afford, make potato salad that was a two-hour project and fix enough other side dishes to feed a small army. (I always wanted to make sure we never ran out of food so I always made way too much.) I could have made iced tea, coffee and lemonade, but I had to have all that, plus four kinds of soda pop.

I hope you're getting the picture that in order for my life to be simpler so it could be enjoyed, I had to change. Life was not going to change; I had to change.

I strongly imagine it will be the same way with you. I suggest that you start to look for all the ways that you complicate things and ask the Holy Spirit to teach you simplicity.

Simple Prayer

I felt that I was lacking real joy in my prayer life, and I discovered that much of it was due to a complicated approach.

First of all, I had listened to too much of what everyone else said I should be praying about. Most people are full of what God has called them to do and what He has anointed them for, and without even meaning to do harm, they get on their soapbox, so to speak, and attempt to get everyone doing what they are doing.

I was as guilty as anyone else in this area, until God got the point across to me that I have to do what I am anointed to do and let everyone else do what He has anointed them to do.

People told me I should pray about government issues — that the government was in such a mess and really needed a lot of prayer. Others said I should pray about abortion, AIDS or the homeless. Missionaries told me that it was missions I should be praying about. Some said I should do spiritual warfare, others said to confess the Word.

I heard people teach on prayer, and it seemed I always came out of those meetings with one more thing I needed to do while praying. People told me how long to pray — it should be at least one hour. People who were early risers told me it was better to get up and pray early in the morning.

Let me say that we will find ourselves praying about all of these issues and for the correct amount of time and at the right time of day for us, *if* we follow the leading of the Holy Spirit in prayer.

I had turned all of my "instructions" from people into laws — things I felt I *had* to pray about. (If you have a complicated approach to the Word of God, it will all become laws instead of promises.) I finally cried out to God and asked Him to teach me to pray, and He taught me some wonderful things that have brought the joy into prayer that is supposed to be there.

First of all, the Lord taught me that I had to pray for what He put on my heart, not for what everyone else wanted to put on my heart. He showed me that I had to pray when He was prompting and leading, for the length of time His anointing was present to do so. He made me see that I would never enjoy prayer if I was in the lead; I had to allow Him to lead me.

The Lord also taught me that I should approach Him simply. This is a very important point. Like any good father, God wants His beloved children to approach Him simply and gently. Somehow I had gotten into doing a lot of yelling in prayer, and although there may be a time for an aggressive tone of voice, I was way out of balance.

I learned that I was not to multiply words and phrases over and over, which we have a tendency to do in order to make our prayers sound impressive. Why can't we learn to simply state our need, ask for God's gracious help and go on to the next thing?

The Lord showed me that instead of praying loud and long, I was to say what was on my heart and believe that He heard me, and that He would take care of it His way, in His timing.

As a result of what I learned from the Lord about praying, I developed my faith in what I call "the simple prayer of faith," as described in James 5:13-15:

> Is anyone among you afflicted (ill-treated, suffering evil)? He should pray. Is anyone glad at heart? He should sing praise [to God].
>
> Is anyone among you sick? He should call in the church elders (the spiritual guides). And they should pray over him, anointing him with oil in the Lord's name.
>
> And the prayer [that is] of faith will save him who is sick, and the Lord will restore him; and if he has committed sins, he will be forgiven.

Sometimes when I simply present to God my need or the need of another individual, it seems in my "natural man" that I should do or say more. I have found that when I pray what the Holy Spirit is giving me, without adding to it out of my own flesh, the prayer is very simple and not exceedingly long.

My mind wants to say, "Well, that's not enough." Our flesh generally wants to go beyond what the Spirit is giving us, and that's when we are robbed of the enjoyment that each thing is supposed to bring.

Let us say that a parent comes to me and asks me to pray for a difficult child. I say, "Father, we come to You in the name of Jesus. I am placing a prayer cover over this family. I ask You to bring them back together. Bring unity between this parent and this child. Whatever the problem is, Father, I ask You to remove the things that need to be removed, and to bring forth the things that need to be brought forth. Amen!"

This kind of prayer is short and simple and really says everything that needs to be said, but the flesh wants to add to it. The carnal mind says, "It's not long enough — not eloquent enough." It required real discipline on my part to go as far as the Holy Spirit was going and no further.

Keep prayer simple, and you will enjoy it more.

Children are always good examples to follow when searching for simplicity. Listen to a child pray, and it will radically change your prayer life.

Simple Desires

Sometimes our desires torment us and keep us from enjoying life. There is a myriad of things that we want, and if we are not very careful, we will strive in the flesh to get them and lose our peace and joy. When we do not obtain the things we want, we get frustrated and upset. It would be much better to simplify our desires than to struggle continually trying to get things.

James 4:2 states, **...You do not have, because you do not ask.** Ask God for what you want and desire and trust Him to bring it His way when the time is right. In the meantime, be content with what you have. (Heb. 13:5 KJV.)

There are two ways to be fulfilled: By working to acquire more, or by learning to desire less. I have learned that the more things that are acquired, the more time is necessary to take care of them. A lot of joy is lost because people have too many things and those things control them.

Occasionally, I go through my house and thin out my possessions. I do not enjoy my home when I collect too many things I don't really need. There is always someone who can make good use of the things I no longer feel are a blessing to me.

The more cluttered your home is, the harder it will be to keep clean. "Clean it out" occasionally, and it will not be nearly as difficult to "clean it up" on a regular basis.

The psalmist David wrote, **Delight yourself also in the Lord, and He will give you the desires and secret petitions of your heart** (Ps. 37:4). Seek God first, desire Him more than anything else, and you will find that He will bless you with what is right for you to have.

If you are unhappy and have lost your joy because of something you desire but don't have, I encourage you not to allow that desire to dominate you. Whatever you do have, you should be in control of it and never allow it to control you.

Suppose a man has a job in which he makes a lot of money so he buys a lot of things — a home, two cars, a second home at the lake and a boat. Then something happens in his company, and he loses his high-salary position.

Say this man secures another very nice job — one that is actually less stressful and more personally satisfying than his previous job, but which pays less. In his new job, he can live nicely on his salary, but he won't be able to maintain the lifestyle he enjoyed on his previous salary.

This situation represents a crossroads place of decision for this individual. He can go out and land a second job to increase his income, or he can try to cut back in other areas in order to reduce expenses.

For example, he might decide that he can no longer afford to take his wife out twice a month as he has done in the past. Although this practice has been very healthy for their marriage, he might decide that the expense is not justifiable so the evening out can be cut from the budget.

In that situation, the obvious thing (at least to me) would be to sell the lake home and the boat. Or perhaps if the boat was very expensive, to sell it and buy a smaller one.

My point is that people are more valuable than things. Peace and joy are more valuable than things. If this man chooses to take a second job in order to maintain the things he owns, he might no longer be able to go to his children's ball games or be there for his wife and family when they need him.

Of course, there are times when having two jobs becomes a necessity for an individual. I am not bringing judgment on anyone who works two jobs, but I am suggesting that all of us need to judge our motives. If something is done out of necessity, it is approved, but not if it is done out of greed.

Many people today are stressed out beyond anything a human being was ever meant to endure, and much of that stress is caused by living in an affluent society that seems to yell continually "You must have more!"

Sometimes I want to yell back, "Stop the world and let me off!" But that only happens when I start letting things and people control me when I should be allowing the Holy Spirit to control my life.

If the Holy Spirit says that something is good, then do it, but if He says no — out it should go.

Always remember that everything you own brings increased responsibility. If you get a bigger house, you will have more house to clean. A bigger car will require more gas. Two cars will mean double insurance.

I heard a gentleman say recently that when he was younger and only had two suits, he never had any stress trying to get dressed for meetings or packing for a trip. The more prosperity he gained in his closet, the more complicated it became to get dressed. Now he has so many clothes to choose from that he no longer knows what he wants to wear.

God wants us to be blessed. His will for each of us is prosperity and abundance. But looking at the fun side of possessions without looking at the responsibility side leads to deception. Getting more things can be fun, but when the fun is over, those same things can be used by the enemy to steal our joy.

Fun is based on what we are doing and getting. Joy comes out of the spirit and often has nothing to do with outward circumstances. Let me give you an example from personal experience.

Recently, a water pipe began leaking in our family room ceiling. The ceiling had to be opened up in two places, which of course was messy. It was not a good time for us. It was close to the holidays, and we were getting ready to leave town for ten days right before Christmas.

The same day, I also discovered that an error had been made on our previous year's income taxes, and we were going to owe some money and have to pay some interest and penalties to cover a mistake that was not even ours.

I did not give much thought to either of the situations. We hired someone to start working on the ceiling, and we trusted that we would have what we needed to pay the taxes when the time came. We even said, "You never know what God may do, He is awesome and works the impossible...maybe this year we will be getting enough back to cover what we owe from last year."

I listened to myself that day. I was whistling, humming, making melody in my heart, and yet I had two big problems in my life at the moment.

Joy is in your heart, and if you won't fill your head with the problem, joy will bubble out. When it does, it will minister to you.

In our case, the pipe got fixed and the mess cleaned up, the holes were patched and the ceiling repainted. Someone who did not even know about our taxes gave us a financial gift that covered what we owed on our taxes with enough left over to pay for the vacation we were going on.

Don't let the devil steal your joy because of concern about things. They can be replaced, or done without — but to be alive and not enjoy life is a great tragedy.

The Simple Approach

Remembering the definition of *simple* as "easy," let's take a look again at Jesus' words as recorded in Matthew 11:28-30. I would like for you to notice how often the words "ease" and "easy" appear in this passage:

> **Come to Me, all you who labor and are heavy-laden and overburdened, and I will cause you to rest. [I will *ease* and relieve and refresh your souls.]**

> **Take My yoke upon you and learn of Me, for I am gentle (meek) and humble (lowly) in heart, and you**

will find rest (relief and *ease* and refreshment and recreation and blessed quiet) for your souls.

For My yoke is wholesome (useful, good — not harsh, hard, sharp, or pressing, but comfortable, gracious, and pleasant), and My burden is light and *easy* to be borne.

First of all, Jesus said, "Learn of Me." I believe He meant, "Learn how I handle situations and people. Learn what My response would be to any given circumstance, and follow My ways."

Jesus was not stressed out or burned out. He was not controlled by circumstances and by the demands of other people.

In John 14:6 He said, **I am the Way.** His way is the right way — the way that will lead us into righteousness, peace and joy. Remember that in John 15:11 He prayed that His enjoyment would fill our souls. That is not going to happen unless we learn a different approach to life and its many different circumstances.

I could write about various things that we need to simplify, and the list would be endless, but if we can learn to have the simple approach to everything, that is far better than learning to be simple in some things.

No matter what you face, if you will ask yourself what the simple approach would be, I believe you will be amazed at the creative ideas you will have.

The Holy One lives in you and although He is awesomely powerful, He is also awesomely simple. The Holy Spirit will teach you simplicity if you truly wish to learn.

I feel my purpose in writing this book is to help people enjoy the life that Jesus died to give them. I know that is impossible without simplicity. I do not feel that I need to teach you all the specifics of simplicity. I believe I am to convince you that you must have it. I want to stir up a hunger in you for it, and help launch you into your personal quest for it.

We are all very different — unique — by God's design. What is complicated for one may be simple for another. That is why it is best for me to teach you the principle and let you find your own road to the destination. When faced with a problem or circumstance, simply ask yourself, "What would Jesus do in this situation? How would He handle it?"

You will find many times that you are trying to handle something Jesus would leave alone. Sometimes I want to confront an issue, and I will hear the Lord say, "Leave it alone."

On the other hand, there will be times when you want to leave something alone and not deal with it, but when you listen to your heart, you know that you need to handle it before it grows into a worse mess.

Sometimes you will want to be part of some exciting thing that is going on, and God will tell you no. Other times, you may prefer not to be involved, and yet the Lord will say, "I need you in this."

You and I will not always or even usually know the "why" behind all of the Holy Spirit's leadings. But simplicity obeys promptly. It is complicated to disobey and have a guilty conscience. Disobedience truly steals the enjoyment of life.

God may tell you no about something at one time, and then at another time allow you to do it. There are no rules except to follow the Word of God and the Spirit of God.

Simplicity and Decisions

But above all [things], my brethren, do not swear, either by heaven or by earth or by any other oath; but let your yes be [a simple] yes, and your no be [a simple]

no, so that you may not sin and fall under condemnation.

James 5:12

Doublemindedness is confusing, yet decision-making can be simple. After making a decision, stand firm, let your yes be yes and your no be no.

I believe indecision and doublemindedness not only bring confusion and complication, but, as James noted, they also cause condemnation.

If we believe in our hearts that we should do something and then allow our heads to talk us out of it, it is an open door for condemnation. We often labor over decisions when actually we just need to decide.

When you stand in front of your closet in the morning looking at all of your clothes, just choose something and put it on. Don't go back and forth until you feel that you don't like anything in your wardrobe.

When you get ready to go out to eat, pick a restaurant and go. Don't get so confused that you feel there is no one place that will satisfy you.

Sometimes I would like the coffee from restaurant A, the salad from restaurant B, my favorite chicken dish from restaurant C, and so on. Obviously, I cannot have it all, so I just need to pick a place and go. Once the food is in my stomach, it doesn't matter where it came from anyway.

Start making decisions without worrying about them. Don't live in fear of being wrong. If your heart is right and you make a decision that is not in accordance with God's will and end up going astray, He will forgive you, find you and get you back on course.

Peter was the only disciple who walked on water because he was the only one who got out of the boat. You may remember that he walked on the water for a while, and then he began to sink and Jesus reached down His hand to him and lifted him up. (Matt. 14:22-32.) Jesus did not leave Peter to drown just because he had done fine for a while and then made a mistake.

Once you do make a decision, don't let self-doubt torment you. Being doubleminded and never deciding anything is complicated. Doubting a decision after it is made will steal the enjoyment of everything you do.

My husband does not mind shopping with me at all, which is a blessing because most men do not enjoy shopping. He gives me a reasonable amount of time to make my choices, but if I go back and forth too many times, he starts wanting to leave.

He says, "Do something. I don't mind being here if we are making progress, but just wandering around and never making any choice is a waste of time."

That does not mean that it is wrong to take a certain amount of time to look things over and search for a good bargain, but if looking and searching go too far, decision-making becomes complicated. Keep it simple. Buy something and move on to the next thing.

I can really get into doublemindedness when I am shopping for other people. At least, I feel that I know what I like, but I am not sure about them. Often I search for the "perfect" gift to the point of losing valuable time. I have done that with my children. Even after all my special effort, they returned what I bought for them.

So, once again, keep it simple.

Just Do It!

Whatever the problem or situation, decision is always better than doubt and indecision.

For example, if you have had a quarrel with someone, it is much easier to *decide* to apologize than it is to stay angry and be filled with unforgiveness, bitterness and resentment while you are waiting for the other person to apologize to you. Be a peacemaker, and you will have a lot of joy.

I spent many years making war, and believe me the price I paid was high. It cost me my peace and my joy and sometimes my health.

Jesus has a way, do it His way and enjoy life.

My husband has always been quick to forgive, and he expects me to be the same way. I can remember him saying to me, "You may as well decide to forgive me now, because this time next week you won't be mad any more and if you forgive me now, it will keep you from wasting all that time."

Indecision wastes a lot of time, and time is too precious to waste. Become a decisive person, and you will accomplish a lot more with less effort.

No one learns to hear from God without making mistakes. Don't be overly concerned about errors. Don't take yourself too seriously. You are a fallible human being, not an infallible god. Learn from your mistakes, correct the ones you can and continue being decisive. Don't fall back into a pattern of indecision and doublemindedness just because you are wrong a few times.

If you feel that God is prompting you to give something away, do it! Get it off your mind. Take some action and sow the seed. If you believe it is right, then do it. That is how you will find out for sure. Devote a reasonable amount of time to waiting on God. Don't follow fleshly zeal, but do follow your heart.

Don't be afraid of yourself! You will not be the first person to make a mistake, nor will you be the last.

The fear of failure keeps thousands trapped in indecision which definitely steals joy and complicates life.

Don't be afraid to make a decision and then follow through on it.

Just do it!

6

Childlikeness

And He [Jesus] called a little child to Himself and put him in the midst of them,

And said, Truly I say to you, unless you repent (change, turn about) and become like little children [trusting, lowly, loving, forgiving], you can never enter the kingdom of heaven [at all].

Whoever will humble himself therefore and become like this little child [trusting, lowly, loving, forgiving] is greatest in the kingdom of heaven.

Matthew 18:2-4

In Luke 18:17 Jesus expressed this same message about the spiritual importance of being childlike when He said, **Truly I say to you, whoever does not accept and receive and welcome the kingdom of God like a little child [does] shall not in any way enter it [at all].**

As we see, *The Amplified Bible* translation of Matthew 18:3 states that the defining attributes of a child are: trusting, lowly, loving and forgiving. Oh, how much more we would enjoy our lives if we operated in those four virtues.

Children believe what they are told. Some people say children are gullible, meaning they believe anything no matter how ridiculous it sounds. But children are not gullible, they are trusting. *It is a child's nature to trust* unless he has experienced something that teaches him otherwise.

71

One thing we all know about children is that they enjoy life. A child can literally enjoy anything. A child can turn work into a game so he is able to enjoy it.

I recall asking my son to sweep the patio when he was about eleven or twelve years old. I looked outside and saw him dancing with the broom to the music playing on the headset he was wearing.

I thought, *"Amazing!* He has turned sweeping into a game. If he had to do it — he was going to enjoy it."

We should all have that attitude. We may not choose to dance with a broom, but we should choose an attitude of enjoying all aspects of life.

The Child in All of Us

Every healthy adult should also have a child in him. Each of us starts out in life as a child, and as we grow up, we need to protect that child within us.

Satan is always out to kill the child, which is why he put it in Herod's heart to issue an order that every male child in Bethlehem two years old and under be put to death. Because Herod was frightened of the newborn Christ Child, the King of the Jews, Whom the Wise Men had come from the east to see and worship, he wanted to rid himself of Him. (Matt. 2:1-16.)

I find it interesting that Satan was afraid of a child, and that a child was the king of the Jews. Kings rule, and perhaps the lesson here, at least in part, is that if we desire to rule and reign as kings in life (Rom. 5:17; Rev. 1:6), we must also become like little children. When we become childlike, it frightens the devil just as the Christ Child frightened Herod.

From Revelation 12:4,5 we can see how Satan seeks to devour the child from the time it is born:

His tail swept [across the sky] and dragged down a third of the stars and flung them to the earth. And the dragon stationed himself in front of the woman who was about to be delivered, so that he might devour her child as soon as she brought it forth.

And she brought forth a male Child, One Who is destined to shepherd (rule) all the nations with an iron staff (scepter), and her Child was caught up to God and to His throne.

Of course, these Scriptures are referring to Jesus, but I believe there is a principle here from which we may learn.

Like many people, I was abused in my childhood. Satan did not wait until I was an adult to try to destroy me — he started early.

Children are not able to protect and defend themselves. And Satan, acting as a bully, often attacks those who seem powerless to fight back. The devil desired to destroy me, mentally and emotionally, as well as to prevent me from ever fulfilling God's plan for my life. He stole my childhood through sexual, verbal, mental and emotional abuse.

I grew up in a dysfunctional home where alcoholism, violence and incest were prevalent. I did not like being a child. As a matter of fact, I hated it. To me, childhood meant being pushed around, taken advantage of, controlled and used. I was very anxious to grow up — it was my predominant thought. I lay in bed many nights and thought about how it would be when I was an adult and nobody could control me.

My plan was to grow up and never allow anyone to hurt me ever again. Of course, this meant that I could not trust anyone, and I had to take care of myself. I did not have the character attributes we listed for a child — trusting, lowly, loving and forgiving. I also had no joy or enjoyment of anything. I occasionally had fun, but never knew any real joy.

I became a workaholic and was driven by the need to succeed. I carried a false sense of responsibility that never allowed me to enjoy anything. I did not know how to do my part and allow others to do theirs. Nor did I know how to let God do His part by trusting Him.

Because of my insecurities, coupled with a determination never to "need" anyone, to me work became an idol. It made me feel that I had worth. I thought God would bless me if I worked real hard.

The Word of God does say that as His beloved children, God will bless us in all that we undertake. (Deut. 28:8.) But we are never to derive our sense of worth and value from what we do. We should know who we are in Christ Jesus, and our work should have value because *we* do it, not the other way around.

In his book, *The Rhythm of Life*, Richard Exley wrote, "There is not enough success in the world to quiet the discordant voices within. Self-esteem is not the by-product of achievement, but the natural consequence of a healthy relationship with one's parents, peers, and, of course, God. It is a matter of who you are, not what you have done."[1]

Work is necessary, and it is good, but if it is exalted to a place in our lives that it was never meant to have, then the good thing becomes our enemy. We often think the enemy is our friend.

I thought work was my best friend. It gave me a feeling of "belonging," as I said previously — a feeling of worth and value. Actually, it was my enemy because I was out of balance.

In *The Amplified Bible* version of 1 Peter 5:8, the apostle warned, **Be well balanced (temperate, sober of mind), be**

---

[1](Tulsa: Honor Books, 1987), p. 36.

vigilant and cautious at all times; for that enemy of yours, the devil, roams around like a lion roaring [in fierce hunger], seeking someone to seize upon and devour.

Areas that are out of balance in our lives are open doors for the enemy. He stalks around looking for these doors. We Christians are often busy fighting demons when what we actually need is the restoration of a balanced life.

In my own case, I needed to work, but I also needed to play. However, I saw no value in play. I actually did not even know how to properly enter into play as an adult, and truly enjoy it. Even when I did fun things, I always had a vague feeling that I really should be working. I actually felt guilty when I tried to relax or enjoy myself.

My experience in growing up had been that I might get in trouble from my father if I was playing, but as long as I was working, my behavior seemed acceptable. I can remember times when as a child I would be outside playing, and Dad would call me to come inside. It seemed that for no reason, he would just make me stop playing. I understand now that unhappy people are irritated by other people enjoying themselves, but I did not understand at the time. I always thought, "I must be doing something wrong."

"He Restoreth My Soul"

He refreshes and restores my life (my self); He leads me in the paths of righteousness [uprightness and right standing with Him — not for my earning it, but] for His name's sake.

Psalm 23:3

I believe that God promises restoration of what is lost or ruined.

I can verify that He keeps His promises.

The Lord has restored my emotions and my mind. My will has been delivered from rebellion. I no longer need to control. I am led instead of being driven — led by the Holy Spirit instead of driven by fear and insecurity.

In my book, *Beauty For Ashes*,[2] I share in detail how this process of restoration was accomplished in my life.

My heavenly Father has also restored my lost inner child. In other words, now I can trust, love, forgive, live with simplicity in my approach to life; and I am free to enjoy what I do. I no longer have to justify fun. I know it is an important part of life and necessary to maintain right balance. I purposely try to enjoy everything I do. I determine to do so.

I take every opportunity to laugh because now I see the value of it, whereas in years past, I might have thought it was frivolous.

The Bible says in 1 Peter 5:8 to be sober of mind. In this context, that word "sober" means serious; however, that does not mean we should be that way continually. In Ecclesiastes 3:1,4 we are reminded, **To everything there is a season, and a time for every matter or purpose under heaven:....A time to weep and a time to laugh, a time to mourn and a time to dance.**

Children are free, and Jesus came to set us free — free to love, to live, to enjoy and to be all we can possibly be, in Him.

In John 8:36 Jesus said, **So if the Son liberates you [makes you free men], then you are really and unquestionably free.**

And in Galatians 4:31 through 5:1 the Apostle Paul wrote: **So, brethren, we [who are born again] are not children of a slave woman [the natural], but of the free**

---

[2]To obtain a copy, see the book list at the end of this book.

[the supernatural]. In [this] freedom Christ has made us free [and completely liberated us]; stand fast then, and do not be hampered and held ensnared and submit again to a yoke of slavery [which you have once put off].

Be determined to have this freedom and to keep it.

You have a blood-bought right to enjoy your life.

Jesus Calls His Own, "Little Children"

I believe one of the ways we maintain our liberty is through frequent reminders of who we are in Christ.

I have noticed that Jesus referred to His disciples at times as "little children." In John 21:1-6, we find recorded a situation in which Peter and some of the other disciples decided to go fishing and had an unexpected encounter with the risen Christ:

> After this, Jesus let Himself be seen and revealed [Himself] again to the disciples, at the Sea of Tiberias. And He did it in this way:
>
> There were together Simon Peter, and Thomas, called the Twin, and Nathanael from Cana of Galilee, also the sons of Zebedee, and two others of His disciples.
>
> Simon Peter said to them, I am going fishing! They said to him, And we are coming with you! So they went out and got into the boat, and throughout that night they caught nothing.
>
> Morning was already breaking when Jesus came to the beach and stood there. However, the disciples did not know that it was Jesus.
>
> So Jesus said to them, Boys (children), You do not have any meat (fish), do you? [Have you caught anything to eat along with your bread?] They answered Him, No!
>
> And He said to them, Cast the net on the right side of the boat and you will find [some]. So they cast the

net, and now they were not able to haul it in for such a big catch (mass, quantity) of fish [was in it].

It seems to me that in deciding to jump up and go fishing, these disciples quickly made an emotional decision that did not produce the desired result. We also frequently make fleshly emotional decisions that do not produce anything until we learn that apart from Jesus we can do nothing. (John 15:5.)

Jesus came to the beach and addressed them in this manner: ...**Boys (*children*), You do not have any meat (fish), do you? [Have you caught anything to eat along with your bread?]...** (John 21:5).

Perhaps Jesus was using this terminology to remind them of their need to come as little children and totally depend on Him.

We see the Apostle John using the same phrase in 1 John 2:1: **My *little children*, I write you these things so that you may not violate God's law and sin. But if anyone should sin, we have an Advocate (One Who will intercede for us) with the Father — [it is] Jesus Christ [the all] righteous [upright, just, Who conforms to the Father's will in every purpose, thought, and action].** He also used this term in 1 John 2:12: **I am writing to you, *little children*, because for His name's sake your sins are forgiven [pardoned through His name and on account of confessing His name].**

Perhaps John learned this expression from hearing Jesus refer to him and the other disciples in this way. It seems to be endearing terminology that immediately puts us at rest, makes us feel loved and cared for and lets us know that we need to lean on the Lord for everything.

If I were to call my son "baby" all the time, it would put an attitude in his mind (even in his subconscious) that I saw him as a baby, and it might even develop in him an attitude of immaturity. I noticed myself calling my boys "son" as they got older. I believe the change of name helped them grow up. They knew I was expecting some maturity from them just because of what I called them.

There are also times when I tell all four of our children that no matter how old they get, they will always be my babies. They know from this that they can depend on us to help them in a balanced way any time they need it. They can always come to us if they are hurting.

Jesus wants us to grow up in our behavior, but He also wants us to remain childlike in our attitude toward Him concerning trust and dependence. He knows that we cannot have peace and enjoy life unless we do so.

We Are God's Children

[And the Lord answered] Can a woman forget her nursing child, that she should not have compassion on the son of her womb? Yes, they may forget, yet I will not forget you.

Isaiah 49:15

Isaiah 49:15 is another Scripture that reveals that our heavenly Father desires us to come to Him as children. In this verse, the Lord used the example of a nursing mother and how she tenderly cares for and has compassion on her child and his needs.

Our heavenly Father wants us to know that we are His precious little ones — His children — and that when we come to Him as such, we show faith in Him which releases Him to care for us.

God is not like people. If people in your past have hurt you, don't let it affect your relationship with the Lord. You can trust Him. He will care for you as a loving Father.

When we do not receive the care and love that we should in our childhood, it causes fears that were never in God's plan for us. Parents are to be a mirror image in the physical realm of what our relationship with God is to be like in the spiritual realm. Frequently, when individuals are reared in dysfunctional homes, it causes problems in their relationship with the Lord.

I pray that as you read these words and meditate on the Scriptures I am sharing, you will experience healing in your emotions that will set you free to be a responsible adult who can come to your heavenly Father in a childlike way — an adult who knows how to work hard when it is time to work, and how to play freely when it is time to play — one who can maintain godly balance in being serious and having fun.

Therefore, Live as Children!

[Live] as children of obedience [to God]; do not conform yourselves to the evil desires [that governed you] in your former ignorance [when you did not know the requirements of the Gospel].

1 Peter 1:14

We must come to God as little children or we will never walk in obedience. We must lean on Him and continually ask for His help. Everything that God has called us to do, He must help us do. He is ready, waiting, and more than willing. But we must come humbly as little children — sincere, unpretentious, honest, open — knowing that without Him and His continual help, we will never walk in new levels of obedience.

In 1 John 4:4 the apostle wrote, **Little children, you are of God [you belong to Him] and have [already] defeated and overcome them [the agents of the antichrist], because He Who lives in you is greater (mightier) than he who is in the world.**

The Greek word translated *children* in this verse as well as many others is partially defined as "darlings."[3]

---

[3]James Strong, *The New Strong's Exhaustive Concordance of the Bible* (Nashville: Thomas Nelson Publishers, 1990), "Greek Dictionary of the New Testament," p. 71, entry #5040.

God wants you and me to know that we are His little darlings.

In 1 John 4:4 the apostle speaks of defeating and overcoming the enemy. Once again, I believe we need to see that this is only accomplished as we come to God as little children — leaning, depending, relying, trusting, etc.

In Galatians 4:19, the Apostle Paul called the believers in Galatia, **My little children, for whom I am again suffering birth pangs until Christ is completely and permanently formed (molded) within you.**

Just as loving parents are willing to suffer for their children if need be, Paul was suffering persecution in order to preach the Gospel to those he called his children. They were ones who had been born into the Kingdom of God through Paul's preaching, and He longed to see them grow up and enjoy all that Jesus died to give them.

In referring to them as children, Paul was letting them know that he was ready to stand by them and do whatever was necessary, including suffering if need be, in order to see God's purpose accomplished in their lives.

A good parent would rather suffer himself than see his children suffer. We see this "parenting principle" in operation when the Father sent Jesus to die for us, His children.

According to the Bible, childlikeness is our God-given, blood-bought right:

> **But to as many as did receive and welcome Him, He gave the authority (power, privilege, right) to become the children of God, that is, to those who believe in (adhere to, trust in, and rely on) His name....**
>
> **John 1:12**
>
> **The Spirit Himself [thus] testifies together with our own spirit, [assuring us] that we are children of God.**
>
> **And if we are [His] children, then we are [His] heirs also: heirs of God and fellow heirs with Christ [sharing**

His inheritance with Him]; only we must share His suffering if we are to share His glory.

Romans 8:16,17

Children are heirs; they are inheritors. Slaves are laborers; they do not share in the children's inheritance.

Are you an inheritor or a laborer?

In Romans 8:21 the Apostle Paul lets us know that God's children have glorious liberty and that one day **...nature (creation) itself will be set free from its bondage to decay and corruption [and gain an entrance] into the glorious freedom of God's children.**

As God's children we were never intended to live in bondage of any kind. We should be experiencing glorious freedom and liberty — freedom to enjoy all that God has given us in Christ. He has given us *life,* and our goal should be to *enjoy* it.

I am not speaking of selfish, self-centered enjoyment that cares only about itself and nothing else. I am speaking of a godly enjoyment — one that learns to have the approach to life and its situations that Jesus had — permitting enjoyment of everything!

Seek to become and remain childlike with all the simplicity of a child. It will enhance the quality of your life in a most amazing way.

A simple approach can change everything.

Try it, you will be blessed!

7

The Complication of Religion

...to as many as did receive and welcome Him
[Jesus], He gave the authority (power, privilege, right)
to become the children of God, that is, to those who
believe in (adhere to, trust in, and rely on) His name....
John 1:12

Jesus has invited us to be in relationship — through
Him — with God, the Father. Relationship and religion are
entirely different things.

In society today the question is often asked, "What
religion are you?" meaning, "What set of doctrines do you
follow?" or, "What set of rules do you adhere to?"

When I am asked that question, I usually respond this
way: "I am a member of a non-denominational Charismatic
church, but I am not religious. I am in personal relationship
with Jesus Christ." Of course, I get some strange looks as a
result of my answer.

Let's examine these two concepts of religion and
relationship to see the important difference between them.

Religion

A portion of Webster's definition of *religion* is as
follows: "Belief in and reverence for a supernatural power
accepted as the creator and governor of the universe...A
specific unified system of this expression."[1] Religion does
not seem to be a very personal thing. There is nothing warm
about the meaning of this word.

---

[1]*Webster's II New Riverside University Dictionary*, s.v. "religion."

Here, religion is described as "a system." I don't want a system. The world does not need a system; we need what Jesus died to give us — we need *life*. Religion does not minister life to us — it ministers death.

Religion is complicated. There is nothing simple about it! It is what *we* can do to follow the system —the rules — in order to gain God's favor.

A woman attending one of my conferences once shared with me the definition she felt God had given her for religion: "Religion is man's idea of God's expectations."

The Pharisees in the Bible were religious. In fact, they were the religious elite of their day, and Jesus called them vipers (Matt. 12:34) and whitewashed tombs. (Matt. 23:27.)

In Ben Campbell Johnson's interpretative paraphrase of some of the New Testament books, he refers to the Pharisees as "rulekeepers." They made sure they kept all the rules, but they had neither mercy nor compassion, nor did they have a godly heart. They were rigid, legalistic, harsh, hard, sharp and pressing. They were exacting. To them, things had to be done a certain way or they were not acceptable.

That is a good description of religion.

Relationship

Webster defines *relationship* as "the state or fact of being related...Connection by blood or marriage: KINSHIP."[2]

I already like the word "relationship" better than "religion" without even going any further. Just reading the definition of relationship makes me feel better. It sounds warmer and friendlier and has more life for me than what I read about religion.

---

[2]*Webster's II New Riverside University Dictionary*, s.v. "relationship."

In Ezekiel 36:26-28, God promised that the day would come when He would give people His heart, put His Spirit in them, cause them to walk in His statutes and bring them into a new relationship with Him:

> **A new heart will I give you and a new spirit will I put within you, and I will take away the stony heart out of your flesh and give you a heart of flesh.**
>
> **And I will put my Spirit within you and cause you to walk in My statutes, and you shall heed My ordinances and do them.**
>
> **And you shall dwell in the land that I gave to your fathers; and you shall be My people, and I will be your God.**

We are now living in the availability of the fulfillment of that promise.

The Lord said that He would take away the stony heart out of man. The Law was given on tablets of stone, and I believe that laboring for years trying to keep the Law — and failing — will give anyone a hard stony heart.

Legalism makes us hardhearted.

Trying, failing, and continually being disappointed leaves us as cold and lifeless as stone, as Paul noted in Galatians 3:10: **And all who depend on the Law [who are seeking to be justified by obedience to the Law of rituals] are under a curse and doomed to disappointment and destruction....**

The Lord has promised that we will be able to keep His statutes because He will give us a heart to do so, and His Spirit to make us able.

The born-again believer does not have to "try" to follow God's ways, he wants to — he desires to. His motives are right.

My response to Jesus is motivated by what He has already done for me, it is not an effort to get Him to do something. I no longer try to please God to obtain His love. I have freely received His unconditional love, and I desire to please Him because of what He has already done for me.

What I have just written is very important. Look it over again and again. For me, it is the pivotal point between religion and relationship.

Religion Versus Relationship

In 2 Corinthians 3:6, Paul said that he and his fellow apostles were qualified **...as ministers and dispensers of a new covenant [of salvation through Christ], not [ministers] of the letter (of legally written code) but of the Spirit; for the code [of the Law] kills, but the [Holy] Spirit makes alive.**

I feel sometimes that religion is killing people. There are so many precious people who are seeking to have relationship with God, and the religious community continues to tell them something else they need to "do" in order to be acceptable to Him.

Don't be offended by my use of the word "religion." I realize that has been a popular, spiritual-sounding word for centuries. I am only trying to present a clear difference between an impersonal set of rules and regulations and a personal relationship with the living God.

Jesus talked of His personal relationship with the Father, and the religious leaders of His day persecuted Him.

It amazes me how certain people always want to come against anyone who talks about God in a personal way or who thinks he has any power from God. It is obvious that Satan hates personal relationship with God and the power it makes available in the life of the believing one.

In certain religious circles, if you and I were to talk about God as if we knew Him, we would be judged and

criticized. People would ask, "Who do you think
Religion wants us to picture God as being f
somewhere up in the sky — unapproachable by any
the elite of the Church. And, further, they want us to believe
that He can only be reached through rulekeeping and good
behavior.

This "religious spirit" was alive in Jesus' day, and even
though He died to put an end to it and bring people into
close personal relationship with Himself, the Holy Spirit
and the Father, that same spirit still torments people to this
day — if they do not know the truth.

I *loved* God most of my life. I accepted Jesus Christ as
my personal Savior at age nine. The tragedy is that I never
enjoyed God until I was in my forties. My entire approach to
Him was religious. It was based on what I could do, not on
what He had already done. I was a "rulekeeper," a modern-
day Pharisee. Not only did I strive to keep all the rules, but I
insisted that everyone else follow my rules also.

When I succeeded, I was proud of myself. And when I
failed, I was condemned. I was attempting to be righteous
(right with God) through my works. I did not yet realize
that all my righteousness would never be enough to justify
me in God's eyes: **For no person will be justified (made
righteous, acquitted, and judged acceptable) in His sight
by observing the works prescribed by the Law. For [the
real function of] the Law is to make men recognize and be
conscious of sin [not mere perception, but an
acquaintance with sin which works toward repentance,
faith, and holy character]** (Rom. 3:20).

The Law was given in order to show man his need for a
Savior. We are supposed to try to keep it until we realize
that we absolutely cannot, and then humble ourselves and
ask God to help us, which He has done in the person of
Jesus Christ.

Religion says, "You have to find a way, no matter how impossible it may seem. You had better do it...keep the rules or take the punishment."

But relationship says, "Do your best because you love Me. I know your heart. Admit your faults, repent of your mistakes and just keep loving Me."

Grace Versus Law

But now the righteousness of God has been revealed independently and altogether apart from the Law, although actually it is attested by the Law and the Prophets,

Namely, the righteousness of God which comes by believing with personal trust and confident reliance on Jesus Christ (the Messiah). [And it is meant] for all who believe. For there is no distinction,

Since all have sinned and are falling short of the honor and glory which God bestows and receives.

[All] are justified and made upright and in right standing with God, freely and gratuitously by His grace (His unmerited favor and mercy), through the redemption which is [provided] in Christ Jesus,

Whom God put forward [before the eyes of all] as a mercy seat and propitiation by His blood [the cleansing and life-giving sacrifice of atonement and reconciliation, to be received] through faith. This was to show God's righteousness, because in His divine forbearance He had passed over and ignored former sins without punishment.

It was to demonstrate and prove at the present time (in the now season) that He Himself is righteous and that He justifies and accepts as righteous him who has [true] faith in Jesus.

Romans 3:21-26

The Apostle Paul had his work cut out for him when he was given the task of preaching grace to the Jewish people of his day. They had been trying to keep the Law for a long time. For centuries they had lived under "the system." When they succeeded, they felt good about themselves, and when they failed, they felt condemned.

As Paul expounded here in Romans 3:21-26, they were having a difficult time understanding the new order of things, so he had to teach them about God's grace which justifies and accepts as righteous all those who have faith in Jesus Christ, Who is Himself the fulfillment of the Law.

After Paul preached this message to the Jews, which is wonderful good news, he told them something that to the religious person is not good news.

Faith Versus Works

Then what becomes of [our] pride and [our] boasting? It is excluded (banished, ruled out entirely). On what principle? [On the principle] of doing good deeds? No, but on the principle of faith.

For we hold that a man is justified and made upright by faith independent of and distinctly apart from good deeds (works of the Law). [The observance of the Law has nothing to do with justification.]

Romans 3:27,28

The flesh of man wants to have something about which to feel proud. It wants credit. In God's new plan, there never would be, and could never be, any credit given to man. Jesus has done everything, and all man is to do is believe!

Everything that man receives from God is attained by faith, not by works.

First the man has to have faith, then he can certainly do good works, but he has to always bear in mind that those "works" do not earn him any particular favor with God. He is to do them from a "pure motive," which is a desire to give, not to get!

Life and Light of the World, Living Epistles

The Church should be bubbling over with *life*. It should be vibrant, alive, active, energized, peaceful and joy filled. I believe with all my heart, as a result of my own experience — in addition to what I have watched other people go through — that a wrong approach to God will totally prevent this kind of vitalized living.

A legalistic, religious approach steals life. It does not nourish it. Remember, Paul said, "The Law kills, but the Spirit makes alive." When we follow the Spirit, we feel alive. When we follow the Law, it drains the life out of us.

The Church of Jesus Christ is supposed to be glorious. (Eph. 5:27 KJV.) Remember, of course, that the Church is made up of her individual members. How can the Church be glorious if those who have accepted Christ as their personal Savior are not glorious?

Each of us should ask the question, "Would people want what I have by watching my life and looking at my countenance?" We are to be the light of the world (Matt. 5:14), living epistles, read of all men. (2 Cor. 3:2 KJV.) As such, our lives are to be letters to the world.

Where Is the Glory in the Church?

Now if the dispensation of death engraved in letters on stone [the ministration of the Law], was inaugurated with such glory and splendor that the Israelites were not able to look steadily at the face of Moses because of its brilliance, [a glory] that was to fade and pass away,

Why should not the dispensation of the Spirit [this spiritual ministry whose task it is to cause men to obtain and be governed by the Holy Spirit] be attended with much greater and more splendid glory?

2 Corinthians 3:7,8

In these verses, Paul revealed how glorious the new dispensation should be by using an illustration from the days of Moses and the Children of Israel.

When Moses came down from the mountain after receiving the Law, the glory of the Lord shone from his face to such a degree that he had to wear a veil when talking with the people. (Ex. 34:28-35.)

Paul used this incident as an example. The Jewish people of Paul's day had already experienced that trying to keep the Law actually ministered death to them instead of life. Paul was telling them that if this thing which ministered death arrived with such glory that it shone forth from the face of Moses, the Lawgiver, how much more glorious should this new covenant be that ministers life?

There are some congregations here and there that are visited with the glory of God on occasion. Are we supposed to wait for God to sovereignly usher in the glory, or should we bring it in with us? Perhaps if we were more glorious personally, we would not need to pray for God to bring the glory. We could bring it with us when we come to church, and take it with us everywhere we go.

If all Christians took the glory of God to work with them, or out shopping with them, or to school with them, it would not be long before the world would be affected in a very positive way.

We believers talk about the glory, preach on the glory, sing about the glory, but the world needs to see it! The world needs to see a lively Church, made up of living stones.

Living Stones

Since you have [already] tasted the goodness and kindness of the Lord.

Come to Him [then, to that] Living Stone which men tried and threw away, but which is chosen [and] precious in God's sight.

> [Come] and, like living stones, be yourselves built [into] a spiritual house, for a holy (dedicated, consecrated) priesthood, to offer up [those] spiritual sacrifices [that are] acceptable and pleasing to God through Jesus Christ.
>
> **1 Peter 2:3-5**

Notice that the writer begins by saying that we must *first* taste of the goodness and kindness of God and "come to Him." Then — like "living stones" — we are to lead a dedicated, consecrated life that will include spiritual sacrifices, but only the kind that are pleasing and acceptable to God.

The only kind of spiritual sacrifices that are pleasing and acceptable to God are the ones that are done out of right motives. They are done to express our love for Him, not to get Him to love us. They are done because of what He has already done for us, not to get Him to do something for us.

God is not for sale!

We cannot buy His love, favor, mercy, anointing, answered prayer or anything else.

The Law Is a Veil

> Nor [do we act] like Moses, who put a veil over his face so that the Israelites might not gaze upon the finish of the vanishing [splendor which had been upon it].
>
> In fact, their minds were grown hard and calloused [they had become dull and had lost the power of understanding]; for until this present day, when the Old Testament (the old covenant) is being read, that same veil still lies [on their hearts], not being lifted [to reveal] that in Christ it is made void and done away.
>
> Yes, down to this [very] day whenever Moses is read, a veil lies upon their minds and hearts.
>
> **2 Corinthians 3:13-15**

In this passage from Paul's letter to the Corinthian believers, we read that when the Law is read, a veil lies over the hearts and minds of the people.

A veil is a separation.

As long as we read the Bible as Law, there will be a separation between us and God that will prevent proper relationship. Even though the Old Covenant is now made void and done away with, if we are legalistic, we will read legalism into everything the Bible says.

Remember, a legalist is someone who is overly concerned with rulekeeping. He exalts rules above relationship.

Don't be a legalist, hiding behind a veil of rules and regulations, but come to God just as you are with open heart and unveiled face.

Come With Unveiled Face

And all of us, as with unveiled face, [because we] continued to behold [in the Word of God] as in a mirror the glory of the Lord, are constantly being transfigured into His very own image in ever increasing splendor and from one degree of glory to another; [for this comes] from the Lord [Who is] the Spirit.
2 Corinthians 3:18

In this verse we read that we must come with unveiled face in order to receive the benefit God wants us to have from the New Covenant.

To me, this means that when I stop being religious and legalistic and just come to Jesus, when I lay aside all "my" works and begin to see Him; when I allow Him to remove the veil from my eyes, then He and I can enter into personal relationship that will ultimately change me into His image.

There is a big emphasis today on spending personal time with the Lord, and rightly so. More than anything else, we need His presence. He is the only One Who can do anything for us that will be permanent.

Unfortunately, many people have been frustrated by this emphasis in teaching. They want to spend time with God, but feel uncomfortable. Or, they don't know what to do during those times.

We must learn to "be," and not always feel that we must "do."

Some express that they never sense God's presence. They have found prayer and fellowship to be a dry experience. I believe one of the reasons is that people are still living under the Law instead of under grace. Grace is not the freedom to sin; it is the power to live a holy life.

But grace also sees when our heart is right toward God and even though our performance may not always be perfect, grace forgives and helps us get from where we are to where we need to be.

The Law condemns. Grace (the dispensation we are now living in) removes the condemnation, and sets us free — free *from* and free *to*. Free from condemnation, self-hatred, self-rejection, fear of God and many other negative traps. And free to serve God without pressure, free to use the life and energy we have been given to behave better, rather than to fight condemnation.

The Veil Removed!

But when Moses went in before the Lord to speak with Him, he took the veil off until he came out. And he came out and told the Israelites what he was commanded.

The Israelites saw the face of Moses, how the skin of it shone; and Moses put the veil on his face again until he went in to speak with God.

Exodus 34:34,35

While I was pondering the veil spoken of by Paul in 2 Corinthians 3, God gave me an awesome example. When a man and a woman get married, the bride comes to the groom with a veil over her face. At the conclusion of the ceremony when the minister says, "I now pronounce you husband and wife," and turns to the groom saying, "You may now kiss the bride," the groom lifts the veil, and he and his bride enter into a more intimate relationship initially depicted by a kiss.

They could never have a close personal relationship if the new bride absolutely refused to take off her veil. Just imagine what the life of that couple would be like together if the bridal veil was never removed.

Even when Moses received the Law and had to place a veil over His face when he was among the people, the Bible states that when he went into the presence of God, he had to remove the veil. Moses could not be in the presence of God with the veil over his face, and neither can we.

Just as no marriage relationship can be proper with a veil between the bride and groom, neither can a relationship between a believer and his Lord be proper until the veil of legalism is removed.

The groom lifts the veil from his bride. Jesus is the Bridegroom, and we are the bride. He has come and lifted the veil of the Law. He has fulfilled the Law for us and paid the penalty for our lawbreaking.

For those "in Christ," the veil is lifted!

Don't be a bride who insists on keeping the veil on, when the bridegroom is trying to remove it. Don't cling to the old way of legalism, but yield to the new way of love.

8

Legalism in Practical Matters

I bear them witness that they have a [certain] zeal and enthusiasm for God, but it is not enlightened and according to [correct and vital] knowledge.

Romans 10:2

A legalistic approach affects every area of life.

I was legalistic with my housework. I cleaned our entire home every day. I vacuumed, dusted, buffed the hardwood floor, shined the mirrors, and washed, dried, and folded whatever laundry had accumulated from the previous day. I had no time to do anything except work, and I resented the fact that I never seemed to have any enjoyment. Without realizing it, I was robbing myself of the enjoyment I so desperately wanted but could not seem to find in my life.

One day some of my friends invited me to go shopping with them. I wanted to go. My heart said, "Yes, go have a good time," but my flesh said, "No, work before fun!"

I was walking down the hall proceeding with my cleaning when the Holy Spirit spoke to me: "Joyce, this dirt will still be here tomorrow. The work will wait for you. Sometimes you have to walk away from it and have a little diversion. I call it the spice in life. Eating bland food will keep you from dying, but it is so much better when it is flavored with a little spice."

Workers and Lovers

A workaholic — which is what I was — gets the job done. Workaholics may even gain the admiration of their peers, but they usually don't enjoy life very much. Also, they frequently start showing signs of the stress under which they live. It shows up on their faces, in their bodies, in their emotions and even in their minds.

"Workaholism" puts a burden on the entire family, and sometimes it places so much stress on a marriage that it ends in divorce.

Occasionally we see a "worker" who is married to a person with a "fun-loving" personality. God brings such opposite marriage partners together to help them maintain balance in their lives. The fun-loving person may need to learn to work a little more, and the worker may need to learn to have more fun.

God's design is that we learn from each other and help fill up one another's weaknesses. We are to keep each other balanced. By watching other people, we may realize that we are out of balance in one area or another.

When a workaholic marries, he may realize that everyone does not love work the way he does. In my case, I was always trying to get Dave to get up and work. He worked all week as an engineer, and on the weekends he enjoyed watching a ball game, going to the golf course or playing with the children. I would nag him to do something "worthwhile." I actually saw no value in enjoyment. I wanted it, but was afraid of it.

In all fairness I must say that I like work, and I am not ashamed to admit it. I am a worker; God fashioned me that way. If He hadn't, this book would not have been written. It requires a lot of hard work to do anything worthwhile, but the good news is that now I also like enjoyment. I have learned to leave my work and enjoy the "spice" in life anytime I feel like things are getting "bland."

Dave was a hard worker, but he managed to enjoy everything he did. I can truly say that my husband has always "celebrated" life. He never even minded going to the grocery store with me and the children. But, if he went, he was going to have a good time. He chased the kids around the store with the grocery cart while they screamed, laughed and yelled with delight.

Of course, I was livid with anger. I would tell him repeatedly, "Will you stop it! Just stop it! People are staring at us. You're making a scene!" None of it stopped him. If anything, it spurred him on. He occasionally chased me with the grocery cart, which really upset me!

Dave is six feet, five inches tall, and he is able to see over the tops of the grocery aisles. He would get in the aisle next to me, and, of course, he could see me, but I couldn't see him. He would throw things over the aisle at me, leaving me wondering what in the world was going on.

I was a very intense person. I did everything with extreme concentration. Going to the grocery store was a major project for me. At the time, we only had seventy dollars for two weeks worth of groceries and a family of five to feed. I was a coupon clipper, so I always had my calculator and box of coupons with me.

In addition, I was health conscious, so I spent a lot of time in the store reading labels to be sure I was not giving my family things that were loaded with sugar or other harmful things.

One day I was extra frustrated with Dave. I was yelling at him, and he finally said, "For crying out loud, Joyce, I'm just trying to have a little fun!" To which I responded, "I did not come here to have fun!" The sad thing was I didn't do anything to have fun. I was not a very happy person.

As I look back now, it is obvious why I was unhappy, but at the time, I was deceived and didn't even know it. I just thought everyone else who did not behave according to my standards was lazy or frivolous.

There were times when we did fun things as a family. I even laughed occasionally, but I never felt quite right about it. As I have mentioned, if I was enjoying myself I always felt vaguely guilty, like I was doing something I shouldn't be doing.

The Bionic Woman

In our society, weakness of any kind is absolutely unacceptable. I used to share that philosophy totally. I somehow felt that as long as I displayed any type of weakness I did not "deserve" to enjoy myself because I hadn't prayed as long as I should have or I hadn't read enough chapters in the Bible that day.

I had "rules" about everything. Things other people did became my rules. Things I heard in sermons or read in books became my rules. I even made up my own rules.

I heard once that even though God gave Moses only ten commandments, by the time Jesus came, the people (especially those with a religious spirit) had turned the ten into at least two thousand detailed rules and regulations. I am not sure where I got all of them, but I do know that I definitely lived under a lot of laws, rules and regulations.

The house had to be clean before I could relax and enjoy myself. My behavior had to be good, and I had to display all the fruit of the Spirit. I had to be a good wife, displaying no rebellion or stubbornness. I had to pray for a certain amount of time and read a certain number of chapters in the Bible. If I overate or ate the wrong foods (unhealthy ones) or did not exercise enough, then I did not deserve to enjoy myself...and on and on the list goes.

One evening, my son asked me to watch a movie on television with him. Basically, he said, "Mom, will you stop being 'spiritual' for one evening and come in here and just have fun with me?" I knew in my heart that he was right, and I decided to do it. But, I did not really enjoy myself because once again I felt vaguely guilty.

I had advanced in my relationship with God far enough to know that the way I was feeling was not correct. I knew there was nothing sinful about watching a good clean family movie with my son. I finally cried out to God, "Lord, what's wrong with me? Why do I feel this way?"

During the next twenty-four hours God began revealing some things to me that were to be life changing. He showed me that the weaknesses inherent in some of the other people in my life had been the open door that had brought in much of my pain and abuse. Personality weaknesses had prevented those who should have helped me from doing so. It seemed to me that weak people either got taken advantage of, or their weaknesses caused other people pain.

I had decided I would not be weak! I despised weakness!

Then I had to face the fact that we *all* have certain weaknesses. We are human. We live in fleshly bodies that get tired. The flesh wars against the spirit, and sometimes we choose to march with the enemy (the flesh). Sometimes we give in to temptation before we even realize what we have done. We have to grow! It takes time! God understands and is willing to be longsuffering, patient, slow to anger, kind and merciful. But we must become willing to accept His graciousness.

Our heavenly Father delights in blessing us, sometimes when we do not "deserve" it. I wanted to earn everything — to deserve everything. And when I did not feel that I had done my part, or my best, then I would not permit myself to enjoy anything.

No one else was doing all this to me.

I was my own worst enemy. I would not permit myself to enjoy anything unless I thought I deserved it!

This revelation from the Holy Spirit was a major breakthrough for me, but I still had to apply it. (Once we see truth, it will set us free, but only when applied.) I began applying my new-found freedom in everyday life. I did my best every day because I loved Jesus, but each day I failed to hit the mark of "perfection."

I began to attempt to balance my life. Work... rest...play...laughter...time with God...time with Dave...time with my children...time with myself. I was learning that, **To everything there is a season, and a time for every matter or purpose under heaven** (Eccl. 3:1). The term "under heaven" means, on the earth.

"Spiritual" Christians
Who Are No Earthly Good

So then, whether you eat or drink, or whatever you may do, do all for the honor and glory of God.
1 Corinthians 10:31

We are on the earth, and there are earthly things that we must tend to. We cannot be "spiritual" all the time. But, if any person has what I call a "religious spirit" about him, he will either ignore the natural things he should be taking care of and create a major problem in his life, or if he does take care of the earthly or secular things, he will not enjoy them.

He will always be rushing through those mundane things, trying to get back to some spiritual activity, because it is only then that he feels good about himself. He only feels approved by God when he is doing what he thinks are "spiritual" things.

We must learn that we can communicate with God while doing the laundry as well as on bended knee. I personally believe God prefers a person with whom to fellowship who talks with Him intermittently throughout the day to one who sets a clock for a certain amount of time. The instant the time is up, he cuts off communication with God until the next day.

The Lord is ever present and always available to fellowship with us or to help us with our needs.

I greatly advocate setting aside special time to fellowship with God and to pray and study. But, in order to enjoy my entire life, I had to learn that He is willing to be involved in everything I do.

According to 1 Corinthians 10:31, we are to do all that we do to the glory of God, which includes the secular realm as well as the spiritual realm. In Luke 19:13 KJV Jesus taught us to "occupy" until He comes. The Hebrew root word from which the term "occupy" was translated means "to busy oneself."[1] I believe that what Jesus meant was that we are to look for His coming with great expectancy, and until He comes, live our lives to the fullest.

God's Presence Makes the Place Holy

And Moses said, I will now turn aside and see this great sight, why the bush is not burned.

And when the Lord saw that he turned aside to see, God called to him out of the midst of the bush and said, Moses, Moses! And he said, Here am I.

God said, Do not come near; put your shoes off your feet, for *the place on which you stand is holy ground.*

Exodus 3:3-5

God called me into ministry while I was in my bedroom making my bed and talking with Him. Making a bed is a rather mundane thing. There isn't anything particularly spiritual or exciting about it, yet God chose to speak to me

---

[1]James Strong, *The New Strong's Exhaustive Concordance of the Bible* (Nashville: Thomas Nelson Publishers, 1990), "Greek Dictionary of the New Testament," p. 60, entry #4231.

about taking a direction that would greatly alter the entire course of my life and my family's lives while I was in my home engaged in this very ordinary, everyday activity.

If you and I will let Him into every area of our lives, we will be amazed at the times and places the Lord will speak to us.

When God appeared to Moses at the burning bush, He told Him to take his sandals off his feet because the place on which he was standing was holy ground. A few seconds before God showed up, it was ordinary ground — now it had become holy ground. His presence made it holy! His presence is in the believer who has accepted Jesus Christ as Savior.

We are God's tabernacle. Our bodies are the temple of the Holy Spirit. (1 Cor. 6:19.) He lives in us! Wherever we go, He goes. If we go to the grocery store, He goes. If we go play golf, He goes. If we go to the park with our children, He goes.

All these ordinary things are things we either must do, or should do, to maintain balance in our lives. The things we do and the places we go in our everyday lives are not holy in themselves, but when we go there and do them, God has promised to be with us. And any place God is becomes holy.

Secular things can become sacred things when the Lord is present. If you and I do all that we do for the honor and glory of God, then it can all be done with an awareness of His presence.

Not all things are of equal value when compared with other things. Some things like prayer or Bible study may be of more eternal value, but that does not mean that God disapproves of the other things or that they are not to be enjoyed.

I believe we should celebrate life, and in order to do so, we must learn to celebrate every aspect of it. All the parts make the whole. Webster defines the word *celebrate* in part as "to observe an occasion with...festivity."[2] Life is certainly a special occasion and should be celebrated with festivities, especially a festive attitude. Our daily confession should be Psalm 118:24 KJV: **This is the day which the Lord hath made; we will rejoice and be glad in it.**

Enjoy Life!

Too often we attempt to be "bionic Christians," and, if we are not careful, we will become so spiritually minded we won't be any earthly good. We read about the great men and women of God in the Bible and Church history who did great exploits. If we are not on our guard, we may begin to feel that unless we are doing great exploits, nothing we are doing is worthwhile.

But we must remember that those people did not do great exploits day in and day out. We hear about the great things they accomplished in the spiritual realm, but they had a secular side to their lives also. They got up in the morning with bad breath just like the rest of us. They had to make a living and deal with unpleasant people. They had to clean house, get along with their mates and take care of their children. And they had to learn to maintain balance; otherwise, books would not have been written about them, because those people probably would have been devoured by the enemy.

When I say that we should enjoy ourselves, I am not promoting carnality. I simply mean that we should enjoy *all* of life.

How many people raise children but never take time to enjoy them? How many millions of people are married and do not really enjoy their mate?

---

[2]*Webster's II New Riverside University Dictionary*, s.v. "celebrate."

In 1 Peter 3:1,2 wives are instructed to *enjoy* their husbands, and Proverbs 5:18 counsels men to *rejoice* in the wife of their youth. There would be a lot less divorce and many more truly happy marriages if couples would decide to enjoy each other and rejoice in each other instead of trying to change each other.

Learn to enjoy people. Enjoy your spouse, your family and your friends. Learn to enjoy your own unique personality and individuality. Don't spend all your time alone, picking yourself apart.

Enjoy your home. Enjoy some of your money *now*. Don't make the mistake of always looking ahead to retirement, at which time you think you will do all the things you always wanted to do in life, but never took the time for.

There is a practical side to life. If we live it with a legalistic, rigid mindset, it will not be enjoyable. Jesus came that we might have life and enjoy it to the full, until it overflows. Do your best to assure that His purpose is fulfilled.

I have always enjoyed what Paul said in Philippians 3:12: **Not that I have now attained [this ideal], or have already been made perfect, but I press on to lay hold of (grasp) and make my own, that for which Christ Jesus (the Messiah) has laid hold of me and made me His own.**

In this reference, Paul was talking about perfection and pressing toward the mark, but I believe this is a spiritual principle that we can apply to all of God's goals for us.

I am determined to enjoy my life — all of it!

I am also determined to live a holy life, develop the fruit of the Spirit, fulfill the call of God on my life, learn the Word of God, have an awesome prayer life and many other things. Some of these latter things may sound more spiritual than saying, "I am determined to enjoy my life," but in God's eyes, I believe they are all important.

Spiritual Burnout

When people get out of balance with spiritual activity they usually experience spiritual burnout.

You and I do not need to be at some church function six or seven times a week, and then spend whatever time we do have at home sitting in a room by ourselves reading the Bible and doing spiritual warfare.

We need balance.

When you ask so many Christians today, "How are you?" the response is, "Tired." Others say, "Busy." *God is not impressed with our fatigue or our "busyness."* Although the Lord has told us to "occupy" until He comes, He has never told us to get so "occupied" that we wear ourselves out.

In Matthew 11:28 Jesus said, **Come to Me, all you who labor and are heavy-laden and overburdened, and I will cause you to rest. [I will ease and relieve and refresh your souls.]** The labor and burden that Jesus was referring to here was specifically the labor and burden imposed on the people by the Pharisees (the religious elite) in their overzealous attempt to keep the Law.

In Matthew 23:4, speaking of the scribes and Pharisees, Jesus said, **They tie up heavy loads, hard to bear, and place them on men's shoulders, but they themselves will not lift a finger to help bear them.**

When is enough going to be enough? Enough will never be enough as long as you and I are dealing with these Pharisee-type religious spirits that work through other people and even our own thoughts and emotions.

Finally, in Matthew 11:18,19 Jesus said of these people, **For John came neither eating nor drinking [with others], and they say, He has a demon! The Son of Man came eating and drinking [with others], and they say, Behold, a glutton and a wine drinker, a friend of tax collectors and [especially wicked] sinners!....**

The "super religious" did not approve of John. Yet when Jesus came and did what they said they wanted John to do, they did not approve of Jesus either. No matter how right we may be, it will never be right enough if we listen to those who make unbalanced demands.

Jesus told the people of that time to come to Him and He would ease their burden and refresh them from their labor. In Matthew 11:30 He added, **For My yoke is wholesome (useful, good — not harsh, hard, sharp, or pressing, but comfortable, gracious, and pleasant), and My burden is light and easy to be borne.** He was obviously saying that the yoke the Law had placed on them was harsh, hard, sharp, and pressing — a yoke they could not bear without burnout.

The same principle applies to us today.

Stop and Smell the Roses

A fine Christian woman recently told me, "I just cannot do it all any longer. I need some time to take care of my dog and my home, and I need some time for myself."

She went on to say, "I feel like all I do is work and run to church activities. I am sick of looking at church people. Sometimes they are so 'super spiritual,' it is nauseating."

She indicated that she wanted to laugh and have some fun, and she was not advocating carnality. She simply was not really enjoying being a Christian, and the cause was excessive spirituality.

She related an incident in which she had invited a man she worked with to a Christian concert. The man was not born again, and she was hoping the concert would be an open door for him to accept Jesus as Savior. She was appalled at how her Christian friends behaved. They had no sensitivity to where he was spiritually.

On the ride to the concert, all they did was talk "spiritual talk" — things like casting out demons — continually using "Charismatic phrases" the man didn't even understand. This woman said, "I was so embarrassed that I wanted to crawl into a hole. I could hardly wait to get away from them."

I don't believe she was embarrassed about witnessing for Jesus, but what her friends were doing was out of season. It was not the proper time for it.

All of these things together had brought her to a place of "spiritual burnout." Once that occurs, people usually want to back off totally, and unchecked, it is an opportunity to backslide.

We need balance!

Satan is into excess. Excess is his playground. If he is successful at keeping us from doing something, his next method is to tempt us to do too much of it.

God has taken time and effort to create a beautiful world for us. What a tragedy to never take the time to enjoy it.

As people often say, "Stop and smell the roses." Even in the midst of work, learn to take five-minute vacations. Stop, look around and take time to enjoy what you observe. Perhaps you will see a child laughing, and it will be a reminder to you of something important.

Sometimes I see an elderly person who reminds me that someday my life will be coming to a close and I should enjoy it now. Looking at a field of wheat reminds me of seedtime and harvest — an awesome principle that our awesome God has established in the earth.

A few years ago, I was in Costa Rica on a ministry trip. We were driving along one day when, all of a sudden, I experienced a sad realization. We had been in some spectacular mountains for four hours, and yet I had not seen them. What was I doing? I was thinking! Probably about how to solve some problem.

I had an opportunity of a lifetime in front of me. The mountains and the countryside were absolutely beautiful, and yet I had not taken the time to even look at them. I was doing "internal work"! That is what reasoning is — "internal work."

As the commercial says, we only get to go around once in life. The Bible says that **...it is appointed unto men once to die...** (Heb. 9:27 KJV). But it is also appointed once to live.

I saw a movie recently in which a man was a workaholic. His life was controlled by working and making business deals and accumulating money. He had a brother who was the exact opposite. He never finished anything in life, was lazy, and did nothing but entertain himself.

Both men were out of balance. The brother who had spent all of his life working had never really enjoyed anything. He had developed no relationships, had never been married; he went through the motions of entertaining, but it was all business to him.

A woman came into his life who recognized his problem — the problem he wasn't aware he had. She loved him, but knew she could never live the way he lived. One evening, after they had gone to dinner, they took a walk. He kept talking to her about work. He took her by a building and said to her, "This is where I work."

She looked at him and said, "I know where you work, but where do you *live!*" She was not asking for his home address, she was trying to make a point.

Take time to live!

9

Too Many Problems To Enjoy Life

We are hedged in (pressed) on every side [troubled
and oppressed in every way], but not cramped or
crushed; we suffer embarrassments and are perplexed
and unable to find a way out, but not driven to despair;

We are pursued (persecuted and hard driven), but
not deserted [to stand alone]; we are struck down to the
ground, but never struck out and destroyed;

Always carrying about in the body the liability and
exposure to the same putting to death that the Lord
Jesus suffered....

2 Corinthians 4:8-10

A great lie and deception from Satan is that we cannot
enjoy our lives in the midst of unpleasant circumstances. A
study of the life of Jesus proves otherwise, as does the life of
Paul, and many others. Actually, they knew that joy was a
spiritual force that would help them overcome their problems.

In John 16 Jesus warned His disciples about many of the
hardships and persecutions that they would face in this life,
concluding in verse 33: I have told you these things, so that
in Me you may have [perfect] peace and confidence. In
the world you have tribulation and trials and distress and
frustration; but be of good cheer [take courage; be
confident, certain, undaunted]! For I have overcome the
world. [I have deprived it of power to harm you and have
conquered it for you.]

Jesus was saying to His followers, "When you have
problems — and you will have them in this world — *cheer
up!*"

113

If one did not understand some things in the spirit, it could almost sound as if Jesus was not being very compassionate. He was really sharing a "spiritual secret": **...the joy of the Lord is your strength** (Neh. 8:10 KJV). Or, as Jerry Savelle says, "If the devil can't steal your joy, he can't keep your goods!"

Joy as a Weapon

[We pray] that you may be invigorated and strengthened with all power according to the might of His glory, [to exercise] every kind of endurance and patience (perseverance and forbearance) with joy.
Colossians 1:11

Paul prayed for the Colossians that they would endure with joy. Why with joy? Because joy enables us to enjoy the journey.

If you and I can never enjoy our lives until the time comes when we have no adverse circumstances, we will live in sadness and never know the joy Jesus intended for us. I also believe that joy, and the expression of it, is a weapon of spiritual warfare, as well as a fruit of the Holy Spirit.

Joy as a Fruit of the Spirit

And you [set yourselves to] become imitators of us and [through us] of the Lord Himself, for you welcomed our message in [spite of] much persecution, with joy [inspired] by the Holy Spirit.
1 Thessalonians 1:6

The believers in Thessalonica were being persecuted for their faith, and yet Paul wrote that they endured the persecution with joy. According to Galatians 5:22, joy is a fruit of the Spirit — not sadness or depression — not frowning or scowling.

If we will remain filled with the Holy Spirit, He will inspire or energize us to be joyful, in spite of our outward circumstances.

I believe the lack of joy is why many times we give up when we should endure. I also believe that the presence of joy gives us the endurance to outlast the devil, overcome our negative circumstances and "inherit the land."

Good Cheer and Good Courage

Be strong (confident) and of good courage, for you shall cause this people to inherit the land which I swore to their fathers to give them.
Joshua 1:6

In John 16:33, Jesus said, **Be of good cheer...!** One definition of the Greek verb translated *cheer* in this verse is, "to be of good courage."[1] When the Lord was giving Joshua direction, He repeatedly told him to be of good courage.

Without the good courage (the cheerful attitude) that God encouraged Joshua to walk in, he would have given up when the enemy repeatedly came against him, and the Children of Israel would never have reached the Promised Land to inherit it.

The same is true of us in our daily walk. Joy and cheer give us the strength to carry on toward the goal that the Lord has set for us in life.

Guard Your Mind, Watch Your Mouth!

This Book of the Law shall not depart out of your mouth, but you shall meditate on it day and night, that you may observe and do according to all that is written in it. For then you shall make your way prosperous, and then you shall deal wisely and have good success.
Joshua 1:8

---

[1]W. E. Vine, Merrill F. Unger, and William White, Jr., *Vine's Expository Dictionary of Old and New Testament Words* (Nashville: Thomas Nelson, Inc., Publishers, 1985), p. 97.

Joshua had plenty of enemies to confront on his journey. As a matter of fact, it seemed there was a never-ending parade of them. But please notice that Joshua was instructed by the Lord to keep the *Word* in his mouth and in his mind, not the *problem*.

Like Joshua, if you and I are to make our way prosperous and have good success in this life, we will definitely need to put our thoughts and words on something other than the problem that faces us. We need to stop thinking about the problem, talking about the problem and, sometimes, we even need to stop praying about the problem. If we have prayed, God has heard.

I am not saying there is not a time for importunity, but often we say we are fellowshipping with God, when, in reality we are fellowshipping with our problem.

In Mark 11:23 Jesus instructed us to *speak to* the mountain. He did not say, *"Talk about* the mountain." If there is a purpose in talking about it, then do so. Otherwise, it is best to keep quiet about it. Words stir up emotions that often cause upset because of excessive focus on the circumstance.

It is valuable to go out and do something enjoyable while you are waiting for God to solve your problem. You may not feel like it, but do it anyway.

It will help you!

Get your mind — and your mouth — off the problem!

Have and Enjoy Life — Now!

We always think we will enjoy life when our breakthrough comes. But what about enjoying the trip — the time of waiting — the journey!

I certainly do not mean to sound negative, but when the breakthrough you and I have been waiting for finally comes, it won't be long until we will be faced with another challenge. If we wait to enjoy life until we have no problems, we may never have much enjoyment.

Let God take care of your problems; cast your care upon Him and do what He has instructed you to do. It almost sounds too good to be true, doesn't it? You can actually *enjoy* life while God handles all your problems!

The Value of Laughter

He [God] will rescue you in six troubles; in seven nothing that is evil [for you] will touch you.

In famine He will redeem you from death, and in war from the power of the sword.

You shall be hidden from the scourge of the tongue, neither shall you be afraid of destruction when it comes.

At destruction and famine you shall laugh, neither shall you be afraid of the living creatures of the earth.

Job 5:19-22

There are some really awesome Scriptures in the Bible about the value of laughter, which is an expression of joy. Job 5:19-22 is one of my favorite passages on this subject. In verse 22 we are told that we will *laugh* at destruction and famine, which is what God would do in a similar situation as we see in Psalm 2:2-4 which speaks of how He handles His enemies.

The Laugh of Faith

The kings of the earth take their places; the rulers take counsel together against the Lord and His Anointed One (the Messiah, the Christ). They say,

Let us break Their bands [of restraint] asunder and cast Their cords [of control] from us.

He Who sits in the heavens laughs; the Lord has them in derision [and in supreme contempt He mocks them].

Psalm 2:2-4

When God's enemies gather together against Him, He sits in the heavens and laughs. He is the Alpha and Omega, the Beginning and the Ending (Rev. 1:8), so He already knows how things are going to turn out. Since He is the beginning and the end, He must also be everything in between.

If we are being led by God's Spirit, we can laugh also during those times. We laugh *the laugh of faith* as Abraham did. God told Him He would do the impossible for him, that even though he was too old to have a child in the natural, He would give him one anyway. Abraham laughed! (Gen. 17:17.)

His miracle did not occur immediately. Years passed by before Abraham saw the fulfillment of God's promise. But I do not think it was the last time Abraham laughed. I am sure many times he thought about what God had told him, and as he looked forward to the day he saw in his heart, he laughed.

We spend too much time in our thoughts looking at what is taking place now instead of looking at the finish line.

Think of all the other things that God has done for you. You had to wait for them also. He is faithful; He will do what He has promised. You may have to wait for a season, but if you decide to enjoy the trip, it will not seem nearly as long.

You may be familiar with the old saying, "A watched pot never boils." When you stand and stare at a pot of water, it seems to take forever to come to the boiling point, but if you go about your business and do other things, keeping your mind off the water, it seems to take only a few seconds.

Watching your problem is like watching the pot of water. If you want to do your part, then get your mind off of your problem. It will be resolved a lot faster and you will be able to say, "I enjoyed the journey."

Laughter as Medicine

A happy heart is good medicine and a cheerful mind works healing, but a broken spirit dries up the bones.

Proverbs 17:22

Laughter not only makes the journey endurable and even enjoyable, it also helps keep us healthy. Worry and anxiety cause stress, which eats away at our health.

The root cause of many sicknesses and diseases is stress. Laughter relieves stress. It alters the body chemistry.

I once read a story of a man who was dying. The doctors said there was nothing they could do. He had his family rent all the funny movies they could find, and he lay in his bed day after day, laughing and laughing. He was completely cured.

I once heard someone say that laughter is like internal jogging. Laughter certainly improves our emotional and mental health, and according to the Scriptures, it has the capability of doing much more.

You may be thinking, "Well, Joyce, I don't have anything to laugh about!"

Many times I don't either, but I have learned to find something. We need to laugh every day as much as possible.

Find Correct Opportunities To Laugh

I have changed a lot in this area recently. A few years ago I probably passed up many opportunities to laugh. I was too busy being serious and intense. Now, when opportunity comes my way, I enter in and get the most out of it. I figure I may as well laugh when I have opportunity, because I don't know how long it will be before I get another opportunity. I know I need to laugh — and so do you.

Laughter and a happy heart must be cultivated. Jesus talked about joy and fullness of joy. I want all I can have of both, but it takes a conscious effort to keep our hearts merry. Satan is always willing to steal or block our joy, and he will do so if we allow it.

Laughter and smiling are outward evidences of inward joy. Often I say, "Some people who are saved need to notify their faces." Some Christians are so sour-faced, they look as if they had been baptized in lemon juice or vinegar.

The world cannot see our heart; they need expression. Our general attitude should be pleasant, abundant with smiles, and if the season is right, we should laugh whenever possible.

There are times when it would be totally inappropriate to laugh. Never enjoy yourself at someone else's expense. Never make fun of another person's flaws. There is a difference between having an anointed good time and engaging in coarse jesting.

Never be rude.

Once when Dave and I took our son to a movie, during the show, Danny said something that struck me funny. I started laughing and trying not to, because I did not want to make a scene. All that made me laugh harder, but I was doing it silently. I laughed so hard that tears were running down my face. Dave was laughing at me laughing, and it was starting to get a little out of hand. Dave said, "We had better be quiet — we are disturbing the other people," and he was totally correct.

Rudeness is never sanctioned by the Holy Spirit.

Suppose I had a relative in the hospital having minor surgery and some friends joined me in the waiting room. We could probably have a good time, but if someone else's tamily members were in there and that person's life was hanging in the balance, it would be rude of us not to consider their feelings.

Make a decision to laugh more, but remember to be sensitive to the timing.

The Climate of Heaven Is Joy

You will show me the path of life; in Your presence is fullness of joy, at Your right hand there are pleasures forevermore.

Psalm 16:11

According to the psalmist, the climate of heaven is joy and pleasure — which means that where God is, there is holy laughter. I have experienced this holy laughter many times while spending time with God. His presence always makes me happy.

The first time I heard anybody laugh with holy laughter, I did not know what to think. I was at an intercessory prayer meeting, and we had been in deep prayer, even weeping and crying out to God in heartfelt petition. Suddenly, we could tell we had made a breakthrough, and the pastor's wife began to laugh.

She laughed and laughed.

We could tell that her laughter was genuine because it was coming out of her spirit. It makes sense to be joyful when you believe you have made a breakthrough.

Why do people tell God how much they believe Him and then spend their days depressed? Remember that Romans 15:13 states that joy and peace are found in believing.

Sudden Breakthrough to Joy and Laughter

The crowd [also] joined in the attack upon them, and the rulers tore the clothes off of them and commanded that they be beaten with rods.

121

And when they had struck them with many blows, they threw them into prison, charging the jailer to keep them safely.

He, having received [so strict a] charge, put them into the inner prison (the dungeon) and fastened their feet in the stocks.

But about midnight, as Paul and Silas were praying and singing hymns of praise to God, and the [other] prisoners were listening to them,

Suddenly there was a great earthquake, so that the very foundations of the prison were shaken; and at once all the doors were opened and everyone's shackles were unfastened.

Acts 16:22-26

This passage relates an account of an incident in the lives of Paul and Silas and how their joy preceded and precipitated a "sudden" breakthrough.

We find these men of God exercising the power of joy in the midst of very difficult circumstances. Their clothes had been torn off, they had been beaten with rods and thrown into jail, and yet they had done nothing wrong. In that depressing situation, they had to be expressing a supernatural joy issuing forth out of their spirits. It could not have been a natural response, because there was nothing in the natural to be joyful about.

Through this incident the jailer was saved. (Acts 16:27-34.) I believe more people in the world will receive the salvation that is waiting for them when Christians begin to truly express the joy of their own salvation.

The Joy of Salvation

And my soul shall be joyful in the Lord: it shall rejoice in his salvation.

Psalm 35:9 KJV

David spoke of the joy that his soul found in the Lord and in His salvation, as we see in Psalm 51:12 KJV in which he prayed after falling into sin with Bathsheba, **Restore unto me the joy of thy salvation; and uphold me with thy free spirit.**

In Luke 10:17-20 we read what Jesus told the seventy He had sent out to minister in His name:

> **The seventy returned with joy, saying, Lord, even the demons are subject to us in Your name!**
>
> **And He said to them, I saw Satan falling like a lightning [flash] from heaven.**
>
> **Behold! I have given you authority and power to trample upon serpents and scorpions, and [physical and mental strength and ability] over all the power that the enemy [possesses]; and nothing shall in any way harm you.**
>
> **Nevertheless, do not rejoice at this, that the spirits are subject to you, but rejoice that your names are enrolled in heaven.**

If you and I had no other reason at all to rejoice, salvation is reason enough in itself for us to be exceedingly joyful. Just imagine how you would feel if everything in your life was perfect, but you did not know Jesus, or, even worse, if you had to face your current circumstances without knowing the Lord.

Sometimes we hear people say, "I feel like I am between a rock and a hard place." When people who don't know Jesus say this, they are being honest; they *are* between a hard place and a hard place. But for those who are in relationship and fellowship with the Lord, they are between the Rock (Jesus) and the hard place. Standing on the Rock is a much better place to be than whatever is available to those without Christ.

Victory is not the absence of problems, it is the presence of power.

God's power is greater than any problem. His victory swallows up all adverse circumstances. We can stand strong, as more than conquerors, when we know that He is with us. Repeatedly the Bible instructs us to fear not, for He is with us. Not only is He with us, but He is with us to deliver us.

Stay Strong by Refusing To Lose Your Joy!

You [Lord] meet and spare him who joyfully works righteousness (uprightness and justice), [earnestly] remembering You in Your ways....

Isaiah 64:5

In the *King James Version* of this verse the prophet says, **Thou meetest him that rejoiceth and worketh righteousness....**

Since you and I are the righteousness of Christ, when we rejoice, God will meet us at the point of our need and see us through to the finish line. A rejoicing heart is not a heavy heart; it is one full of singing. As He did with Paul and Silas in the Philippian jail, God will give us a song in our "midnight hour."

In Isaiah 61:3 KJV the prophet said that the Lord gives a garment of praise for the spirit of heaviness, and in Romans 4:18-20 we read what Abraham did during the time of his waiting for the Lord to fulfill His promises to him:

[For Abraham, human reason for] hope being gone, hoped in faith that he should become the father of many nations, as he had been promised, So [numberless] shall your descendants be.

He did not weaken in faith when he considered the [utter] impotence of his own body, which was as good as dead because he was about a hundred years old, or [when he considered] the barrenness of Sarah's [deadened] womb.

No unbelief or distrust made him waver (doubtingly question) concerning the promise of God,

but *he grew strong and was empowered by faith as he gave praise and glory to God.*

Abraham did not permit his heart to become heavy; instead, he kept up his faith and his spirit by giving praise and glory to God.

I believe Abraham kept a merry heart and therefore his faith was strengthened to carry him through to the end.

Wells of Joy

Now on the final and most important day of the Feast, Jesus stood, and He cried in a loud voice, If any man is thirsty, let him come to Me and drink!

He who believes in Me [who cleaves to and trusts in and relies on Me] as the Scripture has said, From his innermost being shall flow [continuously] springs and rivers of living water.

But He was speaking here of the Spirit, Whom those who believed (trusted, had faith) in Him were afterward to receive. For the [Holy] Spirit had not yet been given, because Jesus was not yet glorified (raised to honor).

John 7:37-39

When we have the Holy Spirit living in us, we have righteousness, peace and joy living in us. (Rom. 14:17 KJV.) Our inner man is like a well of good things. (Matt. 12:35.) One of those good things is joy. But Satan will try to stop up our well.

Actually stopping up the wells of one's enemies was a warfare strategy used in olden days, as we see in 2 Kings 3:19: **You shall smite every fenced city and every choice city, and shall fell every good tree and stop all wells of water and mar every good piece of land with stones.**

The stones of worry, self-pity, depression — all of these things — are Satan's strategy to stop up your well. When your soul is full of these stones, it hinders the flow of God's

Spirit within you. God wants to unstop your well! He desires that the river of life in you flow freely.

Let joy flow! Let peace flow!

Speaking of Isaac, the fulfillment of God's promise to Abraham, we find recorded in Genesis 26:15 that his wells had been stopped up: **Now all the wells which his father's servants had dug in the days of Abraham his father, the Philistines had closed and filled with earth.**

Earth, or dirt, is another thing that Satan uses to stop up our wells. The dirt of judgment, hatred, bitterness, resentment or unforgiveness — the dirt of jealousy and competition. All of these things will definitely stop up our wells and hinder the flow of righteousness, peace and joy.

Isaac reopened his father's wells. Isaac's name means "laughter."[2] He was the child of promise given by God to Abraham and Sarah. They gave birth to Ishmael out of their own works because they grew tired of waiting. Ishmael's name means **God hears** (Gen. 16:11). Genesis 16:11 KJV says that his name will be **Ishmael; because the LORD hath heard thy affliction.** But Ishmael was a man of war. Genesis 16:11,12 (KJV) says of Ishmael: **the angel of the Lord said...he will be a wild man; his hand will be against every man, and every man's hand against him....**

Our own efforts always bring misery and frustration, but God's promise will bring joy and laughter. I believe we can see "a type and shadow" from all this.

Laughter will help unstop our wells!

Maybe you have not laughed — I mean really laughed — in a very long time. You will find that you feel better all over after a hearty laugh.

---

[2]James Strong, *The New Strong's Exhaustive Concordance of the Bible* (Nashville: Thomas Nelson Publishers, 1990), "Hebrew and Chaldee Dictionary," p. 51, entry #3327.

Sometimes I feel as if my pipes have been cleaned out, so to speak, after a good laugh. If I am tired and weary from dealing with life's issues, I often feel like a dusty closet inside — stale and in need of refreshing. When God provides me with opportunity to have a real good laugh, it seems to "air me out" —to refresh me and lift the load off my tired mind.

In Philippians 4:4 Paul wrote, **Rejoice in the Lord always [delight, gladden yourselves in Him]; again I say, Rejoice!** In this verse, we are told not once but twice to rejoice.

When the devil launches war against you, retaliate with joy and laughter, with singing and praises to God. The Apostle James wrote: **Consider it wholly joyful, my brethren, whenever you are enveloped in or encounter trials of any sort or fall into various temptations** (James 1:2). He goes on to say that the final outcome will be good.

Despite your problems, your trials and temptations, be assured that you will benefit in the end, so look to the end and rejoice *now!*

Laughter in Church Services

When God called me to teach and preach His Word, I had no training or experience in the "how to" of developing or delivering a sermon. It surprised me to discover that people did a lot of laughing when I ministered. I never purposely put things into my messages that I thought would be funny, it just happened.

My natural personality, especially at that time in my life, was much more serious and sober rather than humorous or funny. This has helped me to understand that God wants laughter interwoven into the rest of life. We need the serious and the humorous side. Some people have said that laughter helps them handle the correction that the Word often brings.

My teaching ministry in particular is geared toward helping believers grow into maturity, so they can really enjoy all that Jesus died for them to have. This requires correction, dying to self and facing truth that is often painful.

In Hebrews 4:12 KJV we read that the Word of God is **sharper than any two-edged sword** and that it divides soul and spirit. *The Amplified Bible* says that it is **operative**. I like to say that the Word often operates on us, cutting out the "spiritual diseases" that are hurting us. Worship and praise are the anesthesia before the operation, and occasional laughter during the operation is the little extra "calming solution" that keeps us on the operating table.

One person said to me, "This is wonderful; I am laughing while my old nature is being put to death."

It is interesting to me that we sanction crying in church as being a holy and godly response, but laughter in church is very offensive to some people. I think it shows that we need more insight into the nature of God. I believe Jesus laughed a lot more than most of us do.

I have seen laughter spread through a congregation until nearly all the people were laughing hilariously.

One evening in a meeting in Birmingham, Alabama, I had a desire to pray for women who had been unable to conceive and give birth. I was not able to bring the people to the altar for ministry, so I asked them to stand while I prayed for them. There was an obvious anointing on the time of ministry to those standing, and when I finished and told them they could sit down, one woman took her seat and began to giggle.

As I was trying to go on with the service, this woman moved from giggling to laughing and then to hilarity. She was obviously embarrassed and did not seem to know quite what to do with herself. I believe we can control ourselves, and I think if I had told the woman to stop she would have.

I did not tell her to stop because I saw what was happening not only to her, but how it was spreading to others. I felt it was the Holy Spirit so I just stood and watched it. Before long, almost the entire congregation was laughing very hard — I mean hilarious laughter.

You may remember that in Chapter 4 of this book I stated that a compilation of definitions on joy had taught me that it could be anything from calm delight to extreme hilarity. I said that most of the time we live in the calm delight stage, but that the times of extreme hilarity have their value also. This occasion was one of those times.

I found out later that the woman was not from a Charismatic or Pentecostal background. She was not at all accustomed to that type of emotional display in church. The church she attended was much more reserved, and yet God used her, a willing vessel, to usher in "bubbling over joy" for the entire congregation.

Laughter is contagious! I would much rather have someone catch joy from me than sadness. We know that when we are around someone who is depressed and negative, if we do not aggressively resist it, that person's depression and negativeness will start to affect us in a similar way. It is the same way with happy, positive people. They make us feel better, help us forget our problems for a while, and their joy is catching.

I will never forget that meeting, because as I continued to attempt to go on with the service, I was trying to use a Scripture in the book of Job to make a point. Every time I said Job and gave chapter and verse, the congregation would explode with laughter. There were approximately twelve hundred people in the building, and I can assure you, there is nothing funny about the book of Job, yet saying "Job" had the same effect on almost all of them.

Now I admit this is not the normal way our services go, but that particular night, God was ministering to the people Himself in what some would call an unorthodox way. Everyone enjoyed the service. I did not see anyone leave, and I heard a lot of good reports later.

Whenever God has decided to use laughter to minister to the congregation over the years, people have said things like, "I desperately needed that; I haven't laughed like that in years"; or, "I just can't tell you how much better I feel"; or, "I feel as if something heavy has been lifted off of me."

Some have told me even months later, "I have not been the same since that service." Of course, people say that about services where there is no laughter, so I am certainly not implying that laughter is the only thing God uses to bring a breakthrough for His people, but it is not to be excluded either.

According to Ecclesiastes 3:4, there is a time to laugh, so let's not be afraid of laughter — even in church.

A Continual Feast of Joy

...he who has a glad heart has a continual feast [regardless of circumstances].

Proverbs 15:15

One evening I was playing games with some of my family members, and I had been suffering all day with a bad headache. My older son, who has a gift of humor, began to clown around, and I started laughing. I laughed so hard that tears were running down my face, my sides were hurting, and I was close to falling out of my chair onto the floor. What he said was not all that funny. It was amusing, but not funny enough for me to have that strong a reaction. It just seemed like once I got started, I could not stop. When I was finally finished, I realized that my headache was completely gone.

Children laugh easily and freely. As a matter of fact, sometimes, when you watch children play, it seems they giggle almost continually, and over practically nothing. I am sure that they need to grow up some, and that they will as the years go by, but we adults also need some of what they have and display so freely.

Laughter for the average unbeliever is usually based on his circumstances. He laughs only because something funny is occurring or because something really good is happening to him.

As Christians we have a higher privilege, we can laugh even when things are not going as well for us as we would like. The reason we can laugh and enjoy life in spite of our current situation or circumstances is because Jesus is our joy.

In John chapter 15 He teaches us about abiding in Him. Learning to "abide" brings us into a place of rest. It allows Him to do what needs to be done. Just as a limb on a tree abides in the trunk or a branch abides in a vine, so we are to abide in Christ. The branches bear fruit, but it is because of remaining vitally united to the source of their life. We desire to bear good fruit, and the Word of God promises us that we will do so if we abide in Him. (v. 5.)

Then in John 15:11 Jesus said: **I have told you these things, that My joy and delight may be in you, and that your joy and gladness may be of full measure and complete and overflowing.** As we abide in Christ, we should have overflowing joy in our lives. I believe when joy overflows, we will definitely see laughter.

The Proper Balance

There should be a balance between soberness and laughter. The Bible teaches both. First Peter 5:8 says to be **sober of mind**, but it does not say to be sober-faced. Matthew 5:14 states that we are **the light of the world.** You

131

might say that a smile is like the switch that turns the lamp on. There is not much chance of laughter if we do not start with a smile.

If we have a frown on our face, with the corners of our mouth turned down, it almost begins to drag us down emotionally.

When I frown, I can literally feel a heaviness. (Go ahead and try it, I think you will sense the same thing.) But when I smile, I sense a lifting of my entire countenance.

I can be all by myself and smile. I don't even need anything in particular to smile at or about. It just makes me feel happier to smile occasionally even when I am alone. I might add that I have, by nature, always been a very serious-minded, even sober-faced individual, and if I can learn to smile, anyone can who is really willing.

It takes a lot more facial muscles to frown than it does to smile. Some of us probably have weak muscles from lack of use, but they will build up in a short period of time.

Go ahead and try it. Act like a little child. Frown and see how you feel — then smile and see how you feel.

There are two good reasons to learn to smile. First, it helps you look and feel better. Then, it helps those around you.

One of the ways we can show the world the joy that comes from abiding in Jesus is by looking happy. When the peace and joy of the Lord are a regular part of our countenance, it speaks a silent message to those with whom we intermingle.

If you and I go around with a scowl or a frown on our face, nobody in the world will suspect that we serve God. We may have a bumper sticker on our car that says we are Christian, but there is no other visible evidence. We need to look pleasant. We can't giggle all the time, but neither should we look sour.

"Lord, Teach Me To Laugh!"

Pray and believe God to teach you how to laugh more — to help you remember to smile. Start smiling at people and see the response you get, especially from people who look real unhappy or upset. Try giving them a gentle, friendly smile, and it may help them.

I had to exercise my faith in this area for quite some time, simply because I was more sober and serious-minded. I had endured a lot of painful circumstances in my life and, as a result, had formed bad habits that affected my countenance.

Pray, not only that God will teach you to laugh more, but that He will give you things to laugh about.

Are you *under-laughed*? I heard that we need to laugh at least fifteen times a day, three of which need to be hard belly laughs to be at optimum. I can tell you for sure that I was under-laughed, but I am learning.

Remember, a merry heart **doeth** good like a medicine. (Prov. 17:22 KJV.)

Take your medicine — laugh a little more!

10

Diversity and Creativity

And they [the apostles] **went out and preached everywhere, while the Lord kept working with them and confirming the message by the attesting signs and miracles that closely accompanied [it]....**

Mark 16:20

I hope that by the time you have reached this point in the book you are already starting to enjoy life more. I believe whatever we teach on, we can believe God for signs and wonders in that area.

According to Mark, the apostles went everywhere preaching the Word, and God confirmed the Word with "signs and miracles" (**signs and wonders** — Acts 5:12).

I had always believed those signs and wonders to be miraculous healings until God began showing me to believe not only for miraculous healings to confirm the Word preached, but also to believe for and expect miraculous breakthroughs and abundant fruit in whatever area I was ministering. So I am certainly believing that everyone who reads this book will enter into a new level of joy and enjoyment.

There are many reasons why people do not enjoy their lives, and no matter how lengthy this book might be, I could never cover them all. But I do want to be sure that I include teaching on the subject of the vital importance of diversity and creativity in maintaining the "spice in life" which helps keep joy flowing.

Too much of the same things can be a thief of joy.

God Likes Variety!

Behold, I am doing a *new* thing! Now it springs forth; do you not perceive and know it and will you not give heed to it?....

Isaiah 43:19

Do you ever get just plain bored — just really tired of doing the same old thing all the time? You want to do something different but you either don't know what to do, or you are afraid to do the new thing you are thinking about doing? The reason may be because you were created for variety.

I believe God has put creativity in all of us. He is certainly creative and believes in variety. Think of all the varieties of birds, flowers, trees, grass, etc., He has created. People come in a never-ending variety of sizes, shapes and colors, with different personalities.

All of our fingerprints are different. There is not another human being in the world with our fingerprints. The various nations in our world and all the variety of customs and manner of dress are awesome.

Foods and their preparation vary greatly from nation to nation. Italian food is quite different from Chinese or Mexican food. In America, we find the food in the South to be different from that in the North.

God likes variety!

Diamonds in the Rough!

He [God] has made everything beautiful in its time....

Ecclesiastes 3:11

Dave and I were at the Smithsonian Institution a few years ago, and one of my favorite buildings was the one

136

with all the birds of the world in it. Most of the specimens were stuffed, but I walked around and marveled at all the colors, the beauty, the magnificent display of creativity and diversity shown in just this one part of the animal kingdom.

We also visited the gem and stone area, and once again, the variety of gems is awe-inspiring: diamonds, rubies, emeralds, sapphires, amethysts, pearls, etc.

The beauty of the inside of some rocks is amazing. They are crusty and rough-looking on the outside, and yet, on the inside they have unique beauty not found anywhere else. They remind me of people.

We are like that — rough around the edges, crusty and hard on the outside — not much to be desired. However, on the inside, there is a heart that longs after God and greatly desires to be in His will and to please Him.

We are diamonds in the rough!

Diversity and Imagination

And out of the ground the Lord God formed every [wild] beast and living creature of the field and every bird of the air and brought them to Adam to see what he would call them; and whatever Adam called every living creature, that was its name.

And Adam gave names to all the livestock and to the birds of the air and to every [wild] beast of the field....

Genesis 2:19,20

I cannot imagine what kind of a job it must have been for Adam to name all the birds and animals. He certainly had to be creative to do it.

I could go on and on about how diverse and imaginative God was in Creation, but I am sure if you think about it a little, you will agree that our God is an awesome God.

Simply take a walk and look around you. If it will help you, put the book down and do it now. Go rent some nature videos and watch a few. Find out what is in the ocean, or how bees and flowers work together. Then realize that the same Holy Spirit present at Creation is living inside of you if you have truly accepted Jesus Christ as your Lord and Savior. (Acts 2:38.)

There is a lot of creativity inside each of us that we need to tap into without fear.

I think we often get into ruts. We do the same thing all the time even though we are bored with it because we are afraid to step out and do something different. *We would rather be safe and bored than excited and living on the edge.* There is a certain amount of comfort in sameness. We may not like it, but we are familiar with it.

Some people stay in jobs or professions all their lives because what they are doing is safe. They may hate their job, and feel completely unfulfilled, but the thought of doing anything else is frightening beyond words. Or maybe they do think and dream about a change, but their dreams will never manifest because they are afraid of failure, and they will not do their part to see their dreams come to pass.

I do not advocate jumping out in the middle of every "whim" that comes along, but there is a definite time to step out of the ordinary, out of the comfort zone, and into new things.

God has created you and me to need and crave diversity and variety. We are created to require freshness and newness in our lives. There is nothing wrong with us if we feel sometimes that we just need a change. On the other hand, if we can never be satisfied for very long no matter what we are doing, then we have the reverse problem.

The Word of God instructs us to be content and satisfied. (Heb. 13:5 KJV; 1 Tim. 6:6 KJV.) Once again we find that *balance* is the key.

Be Well Balanced

Be well balanced (temperate, sober of mind), be vigilant and cautious at all times; for that enemy of yours, the devil, roams around like a lion roaring [in fierce hunger], seeking someone to seize upon and devour.

1 Peter 5:8

People can definitely get out of balance by doing too much of one thing or another, and when that happens, a door is opened for the devil, as we see in this verse.

Even unbalanced eating habits can open a door for poor health. The Word of God instructs us to do all things in moderation. (1 Cor. 9:25.) We have heard all of our lives beginning in childhood that we need a balanced diet: plenty of good protein, a variety of fruits, vegetables, seeds, nuts and grains, and lots of water.

Eventually there will be a price to pay when we don't obey natural laws. Today, we can take vitamins and other food supplements to help compensate for some of the missing nutrients in our diet, but balance is vital.

Our youngest son dislikes all vegetables. He will eat canned green beans if we make him, but that is about all. I tell him all the time, "Daniel, you need to eat vegetables. You're missing a whole food group that has things in it you need. God wouldn't have put them here if we didn't need them." So far, he has not been moved to change, so I give him vitamins and believe that his eating habits will improve as he gets older.

It is amazing how many people do not like and will not drink water, which is very important for good, lasting health. Often such likes and dislikes are evidence of a certain "mindset." It is something they get into their heads, and until they change their minds, the situation will not improve.

One of my good friends grew up in a family situation in which the dinner table was where the family met to argue. Thus, she grew to hate family mealtimes. She ate a lot of junk food in her late teens and young adult years. She did so partially because she did not want to plan for proper meals.

She did not enjoy thinking about meal preparation, so when she did get hungry, she grabbed whatever was quick. As she grew older, she began to realize that she probably needed to do something to change her eating habits, but she still felt that she just could not be bothered with planning ahead where food was concerned.

Then she had a time of sickness in her life, one severe enough to frighten her, and she *decided* she had to do something about her diet. It was truly amazing how quickly she changed once she had made a quality decision.

This same principle works in anything. People who think they cannot exercise find they can if they decide to do it and stick with their decision. People who have had a lifelong problem with certain issues often find, through the teaching of God's Word, that much of their problem is tied to wrong thinking.

We *can* live balanced lives. Without balance, things get lopsided. There is too much of one thing and not enough of another. Physical sickness, relationship problems and certainly loss of joy can all be the result of unbalanced living.

Taking a good thing out of balance makes it a bad thing. A friend heard that Vitamin E was good and took it by the handful. It was excessively thinning her blood, and she got sick.

The flesh is totally into extremes, and left unrestrained, it will lead to major trouble. The flesh cannot be allowed to have or do everything it wants.

Part of Balance Is Variety and Diversity

When I find a restaurant I like, one that has a certain dish I really enjoy, I am tempted to eat there until I burn out on the place and *never* want to go there again. If I can discipline myself to some variety, however, then I can enjoy the restaurant indefinitely.

Variety keeps the things we enjoy the most in life fresh enough for us to enjoy them permanently. Sameness ushers in staleness, and things we once thoroughly enjoyed are stolen due to a lack of variety.

I find that if I spend too much time with people I really enjoy and delight in, and don't spend enough time with other people, eventually a staleness comes into our relationship.

Dave and I really love each other and we have a great relationship. We are comfortable together, and it is a good thing, because we spend a lot of time together. We work together as well as live together, so we spend more time together than the average married couple. As much as we enjoy each other, sometimes we need to get away from each other. He needs to get out and play golf with his friends, and I need to go shopping and have lunch with one of our daughters or a friend.

We need diversity! It keeps the ordinary fresh.

This may sound like a unique example, but one of the first things God began to deal with me about years ago concerning this subject of boredom and sameness was my pantyhose. You see, I had worn "suntan" pantyhose all my life. Never did I wear any other kind — always the exact same brand and color.

141

I would see other ladies with black, navy blue, creme-colored or even light pink hose, and I liked them, but I kept buying "suntan." God showed me from this simple example that I was sticking with what I thought was safe, even though in my heart I really wanted to venture out and wear something different once in a while.

"Suntan" probably did match most of my clothes better than anything else, and I probably would continue to wear it most of the time, but just a little occasional variety would add some spice to my life and keep me from being bored with my manner of dress.

I am convinced that even if we don't like one thing as well as another, it is still good to incorporate them all, just for the sake of variety. It is a known medical fact that many people who have food allergies are allergic to the things they eat the most. Part of their cure is to rotate their diet.

A friend of mine is dealing with this problem right now. She has been advised not to eat the same thing any more often than once every four days. To rid her body of the allergens, she was instructed to go completely off of what she was allergic to for twenty-one days. After three weeks, she could try adding it back into her diet. But she was told not to eat it more than occasionally or, in some instances, once every four days, depending on how allergic she was to that particular food.

It is very interesting to me to see that God has created even our bodies to demand variety. If we don't give them the variety they need and crave, then our bodies rebel. In essence they say, "I can't handle this. You're giving me too much of this thing, therefore, I'm going to get sick or have some kind of negative reaction every time you feed it to me."

Sickness, pain or other adverse physical reactions are the body's way of saying, "Something's not right." Many times, the thing that is wrong is simply that we are out of balance.

Imbalance and Boredom Cause Problems

Perhaps you are not resting enough or laughing enough, or maybe you are working too hard. Too much stress, frequent emotional upset and a lack of variety in life can all have adverse effects on your health.

God dealt with me about my pantyhose and my eating habits as well as many other things, but the principle is to be applied everywhere. Once you learn the principle of balance, moderation, variety and diversity, you can apply it to relationships, spending, eating, work habits, dress standards, entertainment and many other things.

When we come home from our ministry trips, I love to just be at home — in my house. I prefer to eat at home when possible, and I like to watch good, clean family movies on the VCR or television when available. I like to sit around, or walk around with a cup of tea or coffee and look out the windows. I just like to *be* there.

But, I have noticed that after about three days maximum I start getting bored with what I was loving three days before. There is nothing wrong with me. It is just my God-given nature letting me know that it is time for something different.

I believe God builds these warning signs into us, and if we will pay attention to them, it will keep us out of serious trouble. Our emotional makeup needs change. Denying ourselves necessary variety because of fear or insecurity — or for any other reason — is dangerous. If we do so, we are headed for a great loss of joy.

The fine art of balance is a delicate thing, and each of us must listen to the Holy Spirit and to our own heart. We each have individual needs, and I find it fascinating how one person really needs something that another doesn't need at all.

I have had the same hairstyle for years and years and probably will never change it. But I don't like to wear the same pajamas more than two nights, so I have several pair, and I switch them around so I don't get bored with my nightwear.

My daughter, Laura, on the other hand, changes her hairstyle about twice a year. She tries all kinds of new things — many of which she doesn't like — but she likes change in her hair. Yet, it does not matter at all to her what she sleeps in.

For this reason, we cannot look to other people's lifestyles and choices to tell us what to do. One individual may be totally satisfied eating the same thing for breakfast every day of his life, while another one may want hot cereal one morning and eggs the next, then cold cereal with bananas; one day fruit, then bagels with cream cheese.

Remember that variety means just that, and you are free to have variety within your variety. In other words, you are free to be *you*; you don't have to follow someone else's plan.

Beware of Boredom and Laziness!

Take us the foxes, the little foxes, that spoil the vines....
Song of Solomon 2:15 KJV

I believe that many times people are out of balance, and they don't know it. They are unhappy; they have lost their joy, but they would never attribute it to anything as simple as a need for diversity and creativity in their lives.

We blame our unhappiness on many things, and much of the time that's all it is — *blame*. When we are unhappy, often we want to lash out at someone or something. The truth alone sets us free. (John 8:32.) Many times, we simply need to go back to some of the things God has spoken to us, to the leading of the Holy Spirit that we ignored because we thought it was such a minor thing that it could not possibly make any difference. Remember that the Bible states that it is the *little* foxes that spoil the vines.

Frequently we search for huge monsters in our lives when the answer is simple and right in front of our faces if we would open our eyes and look around us.

We need to repent for a lack of balance in our lives. I do not necessarily mean that we need to get down and wallow in sackcloth and ashes, but I do mean that we need to turn around and go in another direction. We need to be sorry for our wrong way of living and make a decision to change.

Sometimes we are tempted to do what is easy rather than what our heart really wants to do.

For instance, you might get a desire to have some friends over, fix dinner and fellowship, or play games. That is the desire that rises up in your heart, but then your flesh begins to think of everything you will have to do to get ready for that type of evening.

You will need to call the people, go to the store, cook, straighten the house, find the game, serve your guests and then clean up the mess after they are gone. The thought comes, "Oh, forget it, I think I'll just sit down and watch television." Then you are bored and perhaps lonely one more night and continue in the same pattern — joylessly — not knowing what is wrong with you and thinking, "My life is so boring. It's going no place. I can't stand to live like this much longer."

This is where many people really get into relationship problems because, at this point, they blame their dissatisfaction on the person with whom they are in relationship, expecting the other person to provide their joy.

145

People can give us a certain amount of happiness, but they cannot provide our joy.

Joy is a product of the Spirit and the Spirit-led life. If the Spirit is leading you into some diversity, and you remain in sameness out of laziness or for any other carnal reason, it will affect your joy level.

"Television Ate My Friend"

I have nothing against watching television if what is being watched is not ungodly and if it is not done excessively. But I do believe that television is a very large problem for a lot of people.

It is easy to just sit in front of the TV and allow it to entertain you. You don't have to do anything but sit there. However, maybe what you need is not to sit there. Perhaps you are unhappy because you need to get up and exercise some of your creative gifts.

If the abilities God planted in us are not used, they begin to become more and more dormant, and we feel that something is missing, but we may be deceived as to what that "something" is.

I would like to share a story with you that I heard titled "Television Ate My Friend." A little girl had a playmate, and they both enjoyed swinging. They had a contest going between them to see who could swing the highest. They really spent a lot of time together, almost all day, every day.

Well, one of the girl's families bought a television when they first came out, and her mother called her in saying, "Come and see what we bought!" Well, the other little girl never saw her friend again after that. Every time she would go to call her to come play, her friend would be busy.

She would be watching "Howdy Doody," "Captain Kangaroo," "Mickey Mouse Club" or something else. She was always just beginning a new program or finishing one she had started, and for this reason, she could not play. The little girl really missed her friend; they had enjoyed each other so much and had had so much fun playing together. The little girl who was left out did not like television, because she said it "ate" her friend.

Yes, television, if allowed to get out of balance, "eats" people. It "devours" relationships. It can quickly become the babysitter, and be an easy out for parents, simply because they don't want to spend the time with their children that is needed.

Most everyone today is too busy to do the things they really need to do and are spending far too much time doing things that really don't make any eternal or lasting difference.

Television in itself can be a blessing. It is relaxing to sit down in the evening after working hard all day and get involved in an interesting story, but even this enjoyable thing can become a curse if it is allowed to take control or to get out of balance.

Try It, You Might Like It!

I know thy works: behold, I have set before thee an open door, and no man can shut it....
Revelation 3:8 KJV

Perhaps God has been speaking to you about some changes in your life and you want them, but you are afraid. I want to encourage you not to be afraid to step out. Even if you make a mistake, it won't be the end of the world. Don't spend all of your life looking back and wishing you had tried different things, or done things differently.

Wondering what could have been is a lonely feeling. I can promise you that you will not enjoy everything you try. But at least you will have the personal experience of knowing. You won't have to live your whole life hearing about what everyone else is doing and wondering what it would be like.

You are not going to be able to do everything, but step out in God's timing into the things you feel He is leading you into. Go through the doors He is opening. You may even have to take a few steps in some direction and see if a door previously closed will open as you approach it.

For example, God taught me a lesson once using the automatic doors that fly open as someone steps on the rubber pad. He said something along these lines, "Joyce, you can sit in your car at the grocery store all day long, and that door will never open for you. You can watch other people go in and out all day, and it won't get you in the store. But if you get out of your comfortable seat and head toward the door, as you approach, you will find it opening for you also."

Maybe you have a little direction from God, but you don't see the full picture. God leads step by step. He may never show you step two until you take step one.

God is progressive, and I have found that my faith is also. I may have a little faith, and so God shows me a little something to do. Then as I am faithful over the little thing, He shows me the next step, and by then, my faith has grown to be able to handle it.

Maybe you need something simple like taking a different route to or from work.

You might think, "Well, what if I get lost?"

My response would be, "Well, what if you have a good time?"

One of my very favorite eating places is an Oriental restaurant that a friend and I found one day when we set out to look for it. We had heard how good it was, but could not get any exact information about where it was located.

We had some vague directions, and since neither of us are really good with directions anyway, setting out to find it without knowing exactly where it was located made us a little leery about even trying. We had talked about it several times, and each time we talked ourselves right out of it.

But on this particular day, we felt adventurous and decided to take a chance on getting lost in order to see if we could find it. Since we did step out, we found it. As a result of our willingness to step out and "try it," we have enjoyed eating there for years and have directed many others there.

I am not advocating doing foolish things, but I do encourage you to find the balance between living in fear and living with wisdom. It would have been unwise for me to start out after dark by myself looking for that restaurant with no phone in my car. But it was daytime; I had a friend with me and we had a car phone. Basically, our only danger was getting lost and having to ask someone how to get home.

I am encouraging you to introduce into your everyday life as much diversity and creativity as possible. Even when you do the same tasks on a regular basis, try doing them in a different way, especially if you feel staleness starting to set in. You don't have to wait until you are deeply depressed to recognize that you are having problems.

Don't Get Stale and Moldy!

This our bread we took hot for our provision out of our houses on the day we came forth to go unto you; but now, behold, it is dry, and it is mouldy.
Joshua 9:12 KJV

If I have a loaf of bread on the table at dinner, and after dinner, we sit, talk a while and drink coffee, I can reach out and touch the bread that is not covered up and tell if it is starting to get a little dry around the edges. It may not be stale yet, but if I don't wrap it up and take proper care of it, it will soon become hard, brittle and tasteless.

149

The same principle applies to our lives. If we are not careful, the enemy will deceive us into allowing our lives to becoming dry and stale.

Resist the devil at his onset!

Our daughter Sandra travels with us and is the head of the helps ministry in our conferences. When we are home, she helps me in the house. Before she began traveling, she served as our full-time housekeeper, in addition to running the nursery for the local meetings we once held every week in St. Louis, Missouri.

She spent a lot of time cleaning and doing laundry. Anyone who cleans house day in and day out, day in and day out, can get tired of it. It may be one of the hardest jobs to stay excited about, because you clean it and someone else messes it up, and you clean it again, and it gets messed up all over again. This is especially true when small children or teenagers are present.

I noticed once that Sandra was doing jobs on Monday that she normally did later in the week, so I asked her, "What are you doing?"

"I've got to mix this schedule up some way," she answered, "and get a little bit of freshness into it."

You see, sometimes it helps if you just change your laundry day, or, for diversion, watch a movie or listen to tapes while you iron. Try going to the grocery store on a different day, or even better, go to a different store. These simple change-ups can add enough variety to keep things from getting too stale.

My secretary was a perfectionist who has now been liberated from compulsive behavior. In the past, she would never have left her house without the bed being made. She began to see the need for some diversity in her life so she said to me one day, "You are going to laugh when I tell you this."

She went on to say that just for some diversion, she had purposely left her house that morning with the bed unmade. She related that she had thoroughly enjoyed walking out and looking back at it messed up. This was a sign of freedom and liberty for her.

"I will only do it for this week," she said, "but it sure has felt good just to get out of the mold."

When she said that, it occurred to me that *if we stay in the same mold too long, we become moldy!*

Our youngest son, who was eleven at the time and not fond of making his bed or cleaning his room, overheard this lady's story. The next day he said to me, "Well, I'm going to have a little variety today. I'm not going to make my bed."

Of course, he was trying to be funny; he probably thought he had "bed-making burnout," but I wanted him to burn on.

Some people say, "I have to have a routine," or "I'm just a creature of habit." Routine is good, and some habits are also, as long as they don't lead to staleness and moldiness.

You are free to be as routined or habit-oriented as you like, as long as you have joy with it. As a believer, you are free to have **joy unspeakable and full of glory**. (1 Pet. 1:8 KJV). So go for it! Make an effort to see how much you can *enjoy* your life!

Creativity and Diversity in Spiritual Life

The wind [symbolic of the Holy Spirit] **blows (breathes) where it wills; and though you hear its sound, yet you neither know where it comes from nor where it is going. So it is with everyone who is born of the Spirit.**
John 3:8

I have found that when I follow the leading of the Holy Spirit in prayer and fellowship with God, it produces diversity and creativity, which results in freshness and vitality. When I make my own plan, it involves rules and regulations I think will keep me on the right path, but they end up being very dry and boring after a while.

For example, I can make up a prayer list and then pray about those things every day, or I can let the Holy Spirit lead me as He wills. I am not saying that it is wrong to keep a list of things to pray about, but I am cautioning against becoming so list-oriented that the Holy Spirit is left out.

One day the Spirit may lead me to pray more and read the Bible less. The next day it may be the opposite way. Some days I worship and praise more, while other days my prayers are more personal petition. Another day, my prayers are almost all intercession for others.

Some days, I merely sit in God's presence, while other times, I cry for no apparent reason. I will laugh, sometimes, for sheer joy at knowing Him. Or, I may play music and dance before the Lord to honor Him. Sometimes I prostrate myself on the floor and just lie there in worship.

I can promise you that the Holy Spirit is creative; He will never lead us into boredom in any area if we are willing to follow Him. I had to learn, however, that we are often more comfortable with rules and regulations than with liberty.

Many times we are afraid of liberty.

When we make free choices according to the Holy Spirit's individual leading, we must be responsible for those choices, whereas when we do what everyone else is doing, or what the "rules" say we should do, then we will be less likely to be judged or criticized.

There are certain guidelines for many things in the Word of God, and they are the same for all of us, but there is no complete set of guidelines for the "how to" of our personal devotion, Bible study and personal fellowship time with the Lord.

Many of us have such severe difficulty in this area that it prevents us from progressing. We are supposed to enjoy God above all else, not feel dry and bored when nourishing our spiritual life.

Ministry can be a creative experience if we allow it to. The Holy Spirit will lead us in witnessing, giving, exhorting, prayer and literally every aspect of our spiritual life.

We don't have to be in a certain posture to pray.

Sometimes I pray on my treadmill, sometimes and most frequently, in a certain chair in my office at home. It is my place to go in the mornings. But I am not in a rut. If I ever feel that I am, I do something different to stay fresh.

Ministers Need Balance

I have already mentioned how we need to avoid being so spiritual that no one can seem to relate to us. I have had to learn that the rest of my family —although they are called of God just as I am— don't have the *same* call I do.

At one point I thought Dave and our children were very carnal. We would go on vacation, and I was very satisfied to spend a good deal of that time seeking God, but my family wanted to play. I can remember criticizing Dave about not spending what *I* thought was enough time with God. He let me know that I did not know how much time he spent with God, and that just because he didn't do what I was doing, that didn't mean that he was slack in fellowshipping with God.

But he also said a very important thing to me along these lines: "Joyce, I am called by God to be the administrator for Life In The Word and to be your covering. I am very serious about what God has called me to do, but He has not called me to preach."

He said, "I love the Word, and I study, but I do not have the grace to spend as much time praying and studying as you do. You are called and anointed by God to do something, but we don't all have your call and you can't make us prepare for something we are not called to do."

We ministers must be careful about trying to press our families into our molds. In Isaiah 58:6,7 the Lord gives us some good insight into maintaining balance when ministering:

> **[Rather] is not this the fast that I have chosen: to loose the bonds of wickedness, to undo the bands of the yoke, to let the oppressed go free, and that you break every [enslaving] yoke?**
>
> **Is it not to divide your bread with the hungry and bring the homeless poor into your house — when you see the naked, that you cover him, and that you hide not yourself from [the needs of] your own flesh and blood?**

If you are a minister, do not hide yourself from the needs of your own flesh and blood while you are ministering to everyone else.

Several times in my own ministry, a pastor's wife, or the wife of a traveling evangelist or someone married to a person who is called into prison or street ministry, has come to tell me that their marriage is in deep trouble because the minister is never home; he or she is always out doing for everyone else, but never has any time for the family.

You might say, "Well, that's his or her call or job."

While that is true, we all must have godly priorities. God first, family next, work third, then our personal ministry.

If you are called into full-time ministry, you are blessed that your work and your ministry are one and the same. You need time for your own flesh and blood (yourself), and your flesh and blood that is your family. As a minister of the

Gospel, you need diversity and creativity as much as your family does. It will keep you "burning on" instead of "burning out."

Add Variety in Simple Ways

...if only I may finish my course with joy....
Acts 20:24

Adding variety to your life does not have to be expensive or complicated. If you want to do something different in the evening, take the family for an outing. Most young children love to take a ride in the car. Even thirty minutes can be just what all of you need.

Go out and get a cup of coffee. Yes, you could make it at home, but it might not be as much fun. Go get an ice cream cone or a soda. Go for a walk, or sit by the park and watch the children play. During holidays take a ride around the neighborhood and look at the Christmas lights on houses.

If you have a big project in front of you that is going to be an all-day task, take a few short breaks. Walk outside for a few minutes if the weather is nice and drink a glass of iced tea. If you see your neighbors out, talk with them for a while. Go sit on the couch and watch a short program on TV that you enjoy.

You must never lose sight of your goal, but those short breaks can make all the difference in how you feel about the project. It can help you "finish your course with joy."

Whatever you do, if you are obeying Scripture and doing it unto the Lord, you should not only start the course with joy, but also finish it the same way.

11

Joy in God's Waiting Room

A man's mind plans his way, but the Lord directs his steps and makes them sure.

Proverbs 16:9

We think and plan in temporal terms, and God thinks and plans in eternal terms. What this means is that we are very interested in right now, and God is much more interested in eternity. We want what "feels good" right now, what produces immediate results, but God is willing to invest time. God is an investor; He will invest a lot of time in us because He has an eternal purpose planned for our lives.

God sees and understands what we don't see and understand. He asks us to trust Him, not to live in carnal reasoning and be frustrated because things don't always go according to our plan.

Without abundant trust in God, we will never experience joy and enjoyment. We have ideas about how and when things should happen. Not only does God have a predetermined plan for our lives, but He has the perfect timing for each phase. Psalm 31:15 assures us that our times are in His hands. Fighting and resisting the timing of God is equivalent to fighting His will.

Many times we fail to realize that being out of God's timing is the same as being out of His will. We may know *what* God wants us to do, but not *when* He wants us to do it.

157

Give God Time!

After these things, the word of the Lord came to Abram in a vision, saying, Fear not, Abram, I am your Shield, your abundant compensation, and your reward shall be exceedingly great.

And Abram said, Lord God, what can You give me, since I am going on [from this world] childless and he who shall be the owner and heir of my house is this [steward] Eliezer of Damascus?

And Abram continued, Look, You have given me no child; and [a servant] born in my house is my heir.

And behold, the word of the Lord came to him, saying, This man shall not be your heir, but he who shall come from your own body shall be your heir.

And He brought him outside [his tent into the starlight] and said, Look now toward the heavens and count the stars — if you are able to number them. Then He said to him, So shall your descendants be.

Genesis 15:1-5

Abraham had a very definite word from God about his future. He knew what God had promised, but had no word regarding when it would take place.

The same is often true for us. While we are waiting for our manifestation to come forth — waiting for the breakthrough — it is not always easy to enjoy the time spent in the waiting room.

Once God speaks to us or shows us something, we are filled up with it. It is as though we are "pregnant" with what God has said. He has planted a seed in us, and we must enter a time of preparation. This time prepares us to handle the thing that God has promised to give us or do for us.

It is very much like the birth of a child. First, the seed is planted in the womb, then come nine months of waiting, and finally, a baby is born. During those nine months, there is a great deal that is happening. The woman's body is changing to prepare her to be able to give birth. The seed is growing into maturity. The parents are preparing things in the natural for the baby's arrival. They are accumulating the necessary equipment to properly care for a child.

Just as there is a lot of activity inside the mother's body that we cannot see, so there is a lot of activity in the spiritual world concerning God's promises to us. Just because we cannot see or feel anything happening does not mean that nothing is taking place. God does some of His best work in secret, and He delights in surprising His children.

Ishmael Is Not Isaac

Now Sarai, Abram's wife, had borne him no children. She had an Egyptian maid whose name was Hagar.

And Sarai said to Abram, See here, the Lord has restrained me from bearing children. I am asking you to have intercourse with my maid; it may be that I can obtain children by her. And Abram listened to and heeded what Sarai said.

Genesis 16:1,2

Abraham and Sarah got tired of waiting. They were weary and began to wonder if maybe there was something they could do to help things move along faster. In Genesis 16:1,2 we see that Sarah (then called Sarai), Abram's wife, had an idea to give her handmaiden to her husband that he might have intercourse with her. She felt perhaps this would be God's way of giving them the promised child. It seemed to her that God was not doing anything, so she would do something.

Does that sound familiar? During the waiting times, do you ever get a bright idea and try to be "Holy Ghost, Jr."?

Abraham listened to Sarah, did what she asked, and the result was the birth of a child called Ishmael. But, Ishmael was not the child of promise.

Ishmael was fourteen years old when Isaac, the child of promise, was finally born. It probably took longer than originally planned because, once we give birth to the "Ishmaels" in our lives, we have to deal with the repercussions. I always say that once we have Ishmael, we have to change his diapers and take care of him.

We would like to do our own thing and have God make it work out, but He let me know years ago that what we give birth to in the strength of our own flesh, He is not obligated to care for or pay for.

Ishmael never brings us joy. We may love him, because we certainly love the fruit of our labors. What we struggle and labor to bring forth usually means a lot to us, but that does not mean it has the inherent ability to bring enjoyment to our lives.

There are many frustrated people with no joy who head up major works. God did not say we could not build, but the psalmist did say, **Except the Lord builds the house, they labor in vain who build it...** (Ps. 127:1).

It is terribly frustrating to labor and build and have all the visible signs of success, yet be without an ability to enjoy it. We can build, but if our labor is not in the Lord it can be in vain (useless).

Many people spend their lives climbing the ladder of success and find when they reach the top that their ladder is leaning against the wrong building. I don't want to do that with my life, and I'm sure you don't want to do that with yours either.

It is vitally important to realize that whatever God calls us to do, He provides enjoyment for. God has not drawn you and me into relationship with Himself in order to make us miserable. Instead, He brings us righteousness, peace and joy. (Rom. 14:17.)

Many people have no joy from their labors, but this should not be so for the Spirit-led children of God. Enjoying our labor is a gift from God. (Eccl. 5:19.) Enjoyment itself is a gift from God, and a blessed one I might add. I had a position and things, without joy, and I don't ever want it again.

Enjoyment Is a Gift From God

Behold, what I have seen to be good and fitting is for one to eat and drink, and to find enjoyment in all the labor in which he labors under the sun all the days which God gives him — for this is his [allotted] part.

Also, every man to whom God has given riches and possessions, and the power to enjoy them and to accept his appointed lot and to rejoice in his toil — this is the gift of God [to him].

Ecclesiastes 5:18,19

This passage was written by a man who had tried most everything the world has to offer, and he wrote to inform us that the ability to enjoy what we have is a gift from God. But if we give birth to it ahead of time — an untimely birth — it will drain us instead of providing us joy.

Abraham and Sarah made a human mistake. The fruit of their mistake was Ishmael. Because he was Abraham's son, just as Isaac was, God blessed him by making a nation of him also. (Gen. 17:15-22.)

It is good to know that God loves us so much that even when we make mistakes, He can get value out of our blunders if our heart is right toward Him. Yes, God blessed Ishmael, but the promise of God to Abraham could never be fulfilled through Ishmael because Ishmael was Abraham and Sarah's work — not God's.

Like Abraham and Sarah, if we are not careful we may move into the area where we have some of God's will and some of our own, which doesn't work.

Ishmael Cannot Be Heir With Isaac

The Lord visited Sarah as He had said, and the Lord did for her as He had promised.

For Sarah became pregnant and bore Abraham a son in his old age, at the set time God had told him.

Abraham named his son whom Sarah bore to him Isaac [laughter].

Genesis 21:1-3

Isaac was finally born, and he and Ishmael were raised together for three years, but not without some challenges.

In Genesis 21:10, Sarah told Abraham that Ishmael had to go, and God confirmed her words in verse 12 saying, **...Do not let it seem grievous and evil to you because of the youth and your bondwoman; in all that Sarah has said to you, do what she asks, for in Isaac shall your posterity be called.**

Ishmael could not be heir with Isaac. The work of the flesh could not share in the work of the Lord.

There always comes a time when the works of our own flesh must experience death or total separation. God wants us to be inheritors, not laborers. We are heirs of God and joint-heirs with Jesus Christ. (Rom. 8:17 KJV.) An heir receives what another has worked for. He doesn't work himself to obtain what is already his, by inheritance. And if he tries to, he will definitely lose his joy.

I mentioned earlier that Genesis 16:12 KJV says that Ishmael **will be a wild man; his hand will be against every man, and every man's hand against him....** while Isaac's name means "laughter." This really says it all.

When we do our own thing in our own timing and refuse to wait on God, we are going to get war. When we wait for God's promise, it will always bring us joy. The waiting is difficult, but the joy of receiving the prize is worth the wait. How to enjoy the waiting is the key.

God's Way Is Better

For who has known the mind of the Lord and who has understood His thoughts, or who has [ever] been His counselor?

Romans 11:34

We need to come to the realization that God is smarter than we are. His plan really is better. No matter what you or I may think, God's way is better than ours.

I look back now at many of the frustrating times I went through trying to give birth to things in my timing and being frustrated about waiting, and I realize now that I really was not ready for them.

God knew I wasn't ready, but I thought I was. I spent so much of my time asking, "Why, God, why?" and "When, God, when?" I asked questions only God had the answers to, and He had no intention of telling me.

Remember, God wants our trust — not our questions.

I have discovered over the years that trust requires unanswered questions.

When we face puzzling situations, we should say, "Well, Lord, this does not make any sense to me, but I trust You. I believe You love me and that You will do Your best for me at the right time."

God does not need our counsel in order to work; He needs our faith.

In Exodus 33:13 Moses prayed for God to show him His ways: **Now therefore, I pray You, if I have found favor in Your sight, show me now Your way, that I may know You [progressively become more deeply and intimately acquainted with You, perceiving and recognizing and understanding more strongly and clearly] and that I may find favor in Your sight....**

We should pray that prayer regularly, remembering that God's ways include His timing.

God's Timing Is Not for Us To Know

He [Jesus] said to them [the disciples], It is not for you to become acquainted with and know what time brings [the things and events of time and their definite periods] or fixed years and seasons (their critical niche in time), which the Father has appointed (fixed and reserved) by His own choice and authority and personal power.

Acts 1:7

Often we experience a lot of disappointment, which hinders joy and enjoyment, due to deciding for ourselves that something has to be done a certain way, or by a certain time. When we want something very strongly, we can easily convince ourselves that it is God's will for us to have it when we want it, the way we want it.

I always believe for things. I am goal-oriented and always need something to look forward to. Many years ago, I was letting what I thought was faith frustrate me. I attempted to use my faith to get what I wanted. When it did not arrive on time, I felt I had failed in the faith department, or that some demon power was blocking my blessing.

Now, after almost twenty years of experience working closely with God, I know that I can and should use my faith, but God has an appointed time.

"In due time," (1 Pet. 5:6), "at the appointed time" (Gen. 18:14), at "the proper time" (Gal. 4:4) — these are things the Bible says about God's timing. Jesus Himself made it clear that it is not for us to know what these times are.

Remaining expectant every day no matter how long it takes is one of the things that will keep you and me flowing in joy.

When a pregnant woman is waiting to deliver her child, people say that she is "expecting." I am sure most of us are expecting.

I know I am expecting.

There are things God has spoken to me — things He has placed in my heart — that I have not seen manifested yet. Some of them have been there as long as fifteen or sixteen years. Other things He spoke around the same time have come to pass.

I used to be confused. Now, I am no longer confused, I am expecting. My time can come at any moment, any day — maybe today — and so can yours.

Suddenly!

We can expect "a season of suddenlies" in our lives. We can get up in the morning with a major problem and go to bed without it.

God moves suddenly.

Actually, He is working behind the scenes all the time, but just as the birth of a baby comes suddenly, so God manifests what He has been doing for us, suddenly!

In Acts 1:4, after His resurrection Jesus instructed His disciples and other followers **...not to leave Jerusalem but to wait for what the Father had promised, Of which [He said] you have heard Me speak.** They were instructed to wait.

It is hard on our flesh, when God's instruction to us is to wait. There have been times when I have said to the Lord, "What do You want me to do?" And all He said was, "Wait." He did not tell me how long — just to wait.

We must be willing to wait "indefinitely."

In Acts 1:13 we read what the disciples did after Jesus gave them the instructions to wait and then left them behind as He ascended to the Father in heaven: **And when they had entered [the city], they mounted [the stairs] to the upper room, where they were [*indefinitely*] staying....** When they went into the upper room, they did not place a time limit on how long they would wait. They had heard from Jesus, and they intended to obey.

Then in Acts 2:1,2 we are told what happened as they waited: **And when the day of Pentecost had fully come, they were all assembled together in one place, when *suddenly* there came a sound from heaven like the rushing of a violent tempest blast, and it filled the whole house in which they were sitting.**

As they waited — *suddenly* — what they were waiting for arrived.

Just think of it, one minute they were waiting, and the next minute they had the manifestation. That makes life exciting!

We can expect and be full of hope.

A pregnant woman, when her time comes near, goes to bed each evening thinking, "This could be the night." She awakens each day thinking, "Maybe today I will have the baby." She continues in that frame of mind until the blessed event takes place.

We should have that same attitude, and as we do, we will enjoy the trip. We can enjoy the waiting room, but only with the proper attitude.

God Is Passing By!

And Moses said, I beseech You, show me Your glory.

And God said, I will make all My goodness pass before you, and I will proclaim My name, THE LORD, before you; for I will be gracious to whom I will be

gracious, and will show mercy and loving-kindness on whom I will show mercy and loving-kindness.

But, He said, You can not see My face, for no man shall see Me and live.

And the Lord said, Behold, there is a place beside Me, and you shall stand upon the rock,

And while My glory passes by, I will put you in a cleft of the rock and cover you with My hand until I have passed by.

Then I will take away My hand and you shall see My back; but My face shall not be seen.

Exodus 33:18-23

In this passage we see God doing something for Moses that we can definitely learn from and be excited about.

The lesson the Holy Spirit revealed to me from these verses is that we cannot always see God coming, but we certainly know when He has been there.

Moses was hidden in the cleft of the rock, and God hid his view by placing His hand over Moses so he could not see His face.

In other words, we are hidden in the Rock, which is Jesus, and we can rest there while God is on His way to bless us.

We often cannot see Him coming — our situation seems the same day after day — and yet, every day God is getting closer.

Suddenly God passed by, and when He removed His hand, Moses could see His back.

When the wind of God's Spirit blows into our lives, we definitely know that He has passed by.

My ministry team and I see this principle all the time in our conferences, or as a fruit of our radio and television programs or our teaching tapes. People continually tell us that they had such and such problems for years and were set free during one of these events. People often come into our meetings sick and leave well.

A woman with back pain for twenty-four years testified that, after receiving prayer in a Life In The Word meeting, she never had pain again. When someone has had a problem for twenty-four years, that individual is anxious to see God. He passed by in that meeting, and this woman went home healed.

Another woman was carried to the altar because she was violently ill with a migraine headache. Hands were laid on her and prayer offered in Jesus' name. We stood for about three minutes, speaking words of life into her sick body, and *suddenly*, we saw that God's power was affecting her. As a result, she danced out of the meeting, shouting praises to God.

When a person is carried in and dances out, I think we can safely say that Jesus has passed by.

A couple wrote and said that they were on the verge of divorce. Their problems were serious. They saw our television program about relationships and why people don't get along. We offered some tapes on marriage, which they ordered and listened to. God touched them mightily, and now not only are they not getting a divorce, they are both in church and are involved in prison ministry!

I think Jesus passed by!

They did not see Him coming, but *suddenly* there was a major change. Hope replaced hopelessness.

People are living in victory who were previously victims — all because God passed by!

The Lord Will Come Suddenly!

Behold, I send My messenger, and he shall prepare the way before Me. And the Lord [the Messiah], Whom

you seek will *suddenly* come to His temple; the Messenger or Angel of the covenant Whom you desire, behold, He shall come, says the Lord of hosts.

Malachi 3:1

You may be seeking God and waiting on God. Don't give up! God comes suddenly! Your "suddenly" may be today or tomorrow.

God loves you, and He definitely has a good plan for your life.

Believe it! Expect it!

Put your hope in Him, and you will never be disappointed or put to shame. (Rom. 5:5.)

The Silent Years

Jesus spent thirty years in preparation for a three-year ministry.

Most of us might be willing to prepare three weeks for a thirty-year ministry, and even at that, we would rather it not take so long. We are so accustomed to our "instant, everything now" society that we bring these carnal expectations into our relationship with God. It keeps us in a state of turmoil until we see that God is not going to promote us before we are thoroughly prepared.

In His humanity, Jesus went through some things that equipped Him to do what God had called Him to do, as we read in Hebrews 5:8,9: **Although He [Jesus] was a Son, He learned [active, special] obedience through what He suffered and, [His completed experience] making Him perfectly [equipped], He became the Author and Source of eternal salvation to all those who give heed and obey Him.**

Jesus had what I call "silent years," and so did many other Bible heroes who were mightily used by God.

169

The birth of Jesus was recorded in Luke chapter 2. He was circumcised when He was eight days old according to the Law, and shortly after, He was dedicated in the temple, but we hear nothing else about Him in the Scriptures until He was twelve years old. Then, we find Him in the temple sitting among the teachers and asking questions. (Luke 2:41-51.)

The only thing I can find in the Word of God regarding those "silent years" is that He **...grew and became strong in spirit, filled with wisdom; and the grace (favor and spiritual blessing) of God was upon Him** (Luke 2:40).

Between the ages of twelve and thirty, Jesus had more "silent years" — eighteen years when nobody heard anything about Him. He had to be doing something. What? After His parents found Him in the temple when He was supposed to have gone home with them, they took Him back with them: **And He went down with them and came to Nazareth and was [habitually] obedient to them; and his mother kept and closely and persistently guarded all these things in her heart. And Jesus increased in wisdom (in broad and full understanding) and in stature and years, and in favor with God and man** (Luke 2:51,52).

This is another way of saying, "He grew."

Just as Jesus grew during this quiet time, so you and I must grow in many things, and the silent years help provide that growth.

John the Baptist experienced the same thing: **And the little boy grew and became strong in spirit; and he was in the deserts (wilderness) until the day of his appearing to Israel [the commencement of his public ministry]** (Luke 1:80).

Here is a man called by God from his mother's womb to be the forerunner of the Messiah — a mighty man of God — but we hear nothing about him from his birth until the time his public ministry began. What happened during all those years? The Word of God says that he grew. He grew in wisdom and became strong in spirit.

We don't always start out strong. We gain strength as we learn and go through various things. It is a principle of life that everything grows. Faith grows, wisdom grows, along with knowledge, comprehension and understanding. Discernment develops as well as sensitivity to people and to God. The Word of God teaches us, but so do life's experiences, as we see in Proverbs 5:1: **My son, be attentive to my Wisdom [godly Wisdom learned by actual and costly experience], and incline your ear to my understanding [of what is becoming and prudent for you].**

Moses was called, but he needed to learn some wisdom about how to handle what he was sensing: **One day, after Moses was grown, it happened that he went out to his brethren and looked at their burdens; and he saw an Egyptian beating a Hebrew, one of Moses' brethren. He looked this way and that way, and when he saw no one, he killed the Egyptian and hid him in the sand** (Ex. 2:11,12).

Moses did not kill this man based on any instruction from God. He was moved by his emotions. He felt compassion for the Hebrews — he was sensing his call to be their deliverer but he got ahead of God. Shortly thereafter, he encountered two Hebrew men quarreling and fighting; and, once again, he got in the middle of it and tried to bring peace. (Ex. 2:13.)

They took offense and one of them said to Moses, **...Who made you a prince and a judge over us? Do you intend to kill me as you killed the Egyptian?...** (Ex. 2:14). Moses realized that what he had done was known and he fled into the wilderness lands of Midian. He married and lived there for forty years. During those years we hear nothing much about him. They were "silent years."

But then came the burning bush incident in which God told Moses what He was called to do. The Bible reports that when God called Moses, he was at that time the meekest man on the face of the earth. (Num. 12:3.) Something had happened to him during those silent years. I believe he was getting his equipment. He was being prepared for the call that had always been there.

Joseph had a dream he shared with his brothers, who became offended. They were jealous, but many of us might have been also. Joseph probably should have used more wisdom and pondered the things he dreamed in his own heart. I doubt that many brothers would be excited if one of them announced to the others, "I saw you all bowing down to me." How could Joseph use wisdom he did not have yet? Gaining wisdom requires time and experience.

You probably know the story. Joseph's brothers sold him into slavery, but told their father that he had been killed by a wild animal. As a slave, Joseph was taken to Egypt, and because God's favor was on him, he was placed in a position of authority everywhere he turned.

He even spent years in prison for doing something for which he was not guilty; but God was with him through it all. At the appointed time, God promoted him, and he finally had so much authority that only Pharaoh himself had more authority in the land than Joseph.

Believe me, when our time comes, no devil in hell and no person on earth will be able to prevent God from promoting and blessing us. But if we try to get where we are going ahead of time, it simply does not work. We will be miserable, and, we will hinder God — not help Him.

There is an appointed time. Only God knows exactly when it is, so settle down and enjoy the trip.

Enjoy where you are on the way to where you are going!

172

I remember the "silent years" in my life — years when I knew I had a call into ministry — but nothing was happening. Those were years when I was believing but not seeing.

We all have times when we feel that nothing is happening and it seems that no one, not even God, really even cares. We can't seem to hear from God. We can't "feel" God. We wonder if we are a little "flaky," or maybe we never heard from God after all.

Those are times when it seems as if God has placed us neatly on a shelf, and we wonder if He will ever use us, or if we will ever experience our breakthrough.

Waiting! Waiting! Waiting!

It sometimes seems to us that we have waited forever. We grow weary and don't feel that we can hang on much longer, and then, something happens — maybe just a little something.

Like the Prophet Elijah, we see a cloud the size of a man's hand on the horizon (1 Kings 18:44), and it gives us confidence that it really is going to rain.

Perhaps your "cloud" is a special word from God that someone gives you, or perhaps you are touched by God in a specific way. Perhaps a gift comes — something for which you have been believing — that only God knew about, and it encourages you that the Lord knows that you are alive and waiting.

Maybe you are called to preach and receive an invitation to speak at the men's fellowship or the women's prayer group at church. The invitation renews your hope that doors are beginning to open.

I literally watched God do this type of thing for me for years. I had such a big vision, and I was consumed with it. I was "pregnant" with a dream. Had I really heard from God or was I making it up? I was teaching a Bible study, but I wanted — and felt called — to do so much more.

The "silent years" were very difficult, but very necessary. I was growing, gaining wisdom, experience, learning how to come under authority, learning the Word that I was called to preach.

Many people would like to preach, but they don't even have a message.

Just when I was about ready to give up, the wind of God would blow by. He would do something to keep me hoping.

God is closely watching over the lives of His children, and He will never allow more to come on us than we can bear. (1 Cor. 10:13.) God provides the way out of every situation in due time. In the meantime, He will give us what we need to be stable and joyful if we will trust Him for it, realizing that He knows best.

Preparation

Remind people to be submissive to [their] magistrates and authorities, to be obedient, *to be prepared* and willing to do any upright and honorable work.

Titus 3:1

In Luke 3:1-6 God sent John the Baptist to proclaim to the people, ...*Prepare* **the way of the Lord...** (v. 4). In John 14:2 when Jesus was getting ready to leave the earth, He told His disciples: ...**I am going away to** *prepare* **a place for you.** In Matthew 20:23, when the mother of Zebedee's children came to Jesus asking that her two sons be permitted to sit one on His right hand, and one on His left, **He said to them, You will drink My cup, but seats at My right hand and at My left are not Mine to give, but they are for those for whom they have been ordained and** *prepared* **by My Father.**

We get the picture quickly that God does not do anything without first being prepared, and neither will He allow us to do His work without adequate preparation.

In Titus 3:1, Paul wrote, "Be prepared for any upright and honorable work." And in 2 Timothy 2:15 he instructed his young disciple: **Study and be eager and do your utmost to present yourself to God approved (tested by trial), a workman who has no cause to be ashamed, correctly analyzing and accurately dividing [rightly handling and skillfully teaching] the Word of Truth.**

Your preparation may mean going to Bible college or getting some other kind of formal training, or it may mean spending a few years working under someone else's authority in ministry so you will know how to handle yourself down the road. It could mean working at a job that you don't particularly like, for a boss of whom you are not very fond.

It could also mean spending some years in which your basic needs are met, but you are definitely not living in abundance because you are learning how to believe God for prosperity and how to handle it when you get it.

Many desire to prosper, but not all want to prepare to prosper.

Preparation may take place in a lot of different settings, but the fact remains that we must be prepared.

Each phase we go through is important. There is something to be learned at every step. It is all part of our preparation. We must "graduate," so to speak, from each phase or level into the next one, and this comes after we have proven ourselves on the current level. Between all of these stages of preparation, there is a lot of waiting.

Unless we learn to wait well, we will be miserable little saints. Miserable people are usually grouchy, critical and just generally hard to get along with. Miserable people usually make other people miserable.

Enjoy the trip! Being miserable will not make it any shorter, but it could make it longer.

"Have a Seat"

And He [God] raised us up together with Him [Christ] and made us sit down together [giving us joint seating with Him] in the heavenly sphere [by virtue of our being] in Christ Jesus (the Messiah, the Anointed One).

Ephesians 2:6

If you have an appointment with a doctor, dentist, lawyer, etc., when you arrive at the office usually the first thing the receptionist says to you is, "Have a seat. We will be with you soon." The offering of a seat is an invitation to rest while you are waiting.

There will probably be a selection of magazines to read or a television to watch. These are provided to give you something to take your mind off the waiting. If you are busy doing something, the time will go by faster. The person you have come to see wants you to enjoy the wait and not be frustrated by it.

When Jesus finished His work, He ascended on high and the Bible records that He sat down. His work was finished, so He entered the state of rest. Most New Testament references to Jesus in heaven after His ascension, depict Him as seated, as in Hebrews 1:13, **Besides, to which of the angels has He [God] ever said, Sit at My right hand [associated with Me in My royal dignity] till I make your enemies a stool for your feet?**

Jesus has finished what His Father sent Him to do. Now, He is being told to "have a seat and rest until I take care of Your enemies." We must understand that the same offer is available to us. According to Ephesians 2:6, we are seated in heavenly places in Christ Jesus!

When we go into the waiting room to wait for any appointment, we are offered a seat. If we choose to, we can pace around, wringing our hands, checking every few seconds to see if the person we want to meet is ready for us. But there is another choice. We can have a seat and do something to make the wait enjoyable.

"Let Nature Take Its Course"

This is a phrase we often hear, which is another way of saying, "Settle down and let things happen according to the prescribed timetable."

With each of our four children, I was pregnant ten months. After the birth of the fourth one, my doctor finally said, "You are the only woman I know who stays pregnant as long as an elephant."

Needless to say, it was a difficult experience. Who knows? Maybe God was trying to teach me, even back then, how to wait properly.

We never learn patience without something to be patient about. Patience is something that has to be worked in us — it doesn't just appear.

The fruit of patience is in our spirits, because as children of God, the Holy Spirit is resident within us. But for patience to be expressed through our souls (our mind, will and emotions), a work must be done in us.

Once the prescribed time of waiting for the birth of each of my children had passed, I tried everything imaginable to bring on labor. I walked, took castor oil, worked harder than usual, hoping it would help "speed things up." With one of them, I even went into the hospital so the doctor would induce labor. It didn't work; I was sent home. The doctor basically said, "Go home and let nature take its course."

My advice to you from the Word of God and from my experience in life is, "Don't be in such a big hurry." You may be "pregnant" with dreams for your life, but you may also be trying to have your "baby" out of season.

We can make huge messes in our lives, and sometimes get upset with God because things didn't work out the way we thought the Lord said they would. Things will happen as God said *if* we wait on His timing. We are the ones in a hurry. God is not in a hurry!

In Psalm 37:4 we are told: **Delight yourself also in the Lord, and He will give you the desires and secret petitions of your heart.**

Stay busy delighting yourself in the Lord, and let Him give you what He wants you to have. If God has placed the desire in you, you can be assured that He will bring it to birth in the right season. Wait on God for direction and instruction on how to proceed, do what He tells you or shows you, but don't go beyond that.

Learn to "Wait Well"

...See how the farmer waits expectantly for the precious harvest from the land. [See how] he keeps up his patient [vigil] over it until it receives the early and late rains.

So you also must be patient....

James 5:7,8

Learn to wait patiently. That really means learn to wait with a good attitude.

I have learned that patience is not my ability to wait, it is how I act while I am waiting.

We are going to wait no matter what we do. Waiting is a fact of life. We actually spend more time waiting than we do receiving. Our attitude, and how we act during the wait, will determine whether we enjoy the trip. It will also help determine the length of the trip.

All the things we should be doing while we are waiting are the exact reason why we must wait. I encourage you to think about that statement: All the wrong things we do while we are waiting — things like giving birth to "Ishmaels," having bad attitudes, being jealous of others who already have what we are waiting for, attending "pity parties" on a regular basis, being on an emotional roller coaster — all these things and more are exactly why we have to wait. They must be dealt with — worked out of us. The simple fact is that preparation is a process requiring time.

Even when we are more mature and ready for some of God's best, we may be waiting for God to deal with the other people who will be involved with us. There is a multi-faceted work that God is doing — an intricate work — and we are better off to leave it alone and let God be God!

There is a purifying work that must be done in our lives to fit and equip us for the thing God has stored up for us, the thing He has put in our heart.

Possibly, most people never come into the fullness of what God has for them. They never see the fulfillment of their dreams and visions simply because they either don't understand the things shared in this book, or they do understand, and are just plain stubborn and rebellious.

Yes, this inability to "wait well" is one of the major reasons why people don't enjoy their lives. But, I believe you will be changed as you read this book. Remember, we are expecting signs and wonders in this area to confirm the word being taught.

Here is an example that may help.

When God called us to begin a television ministry in 1993 we accepted the call and the responsibility that went with it. The first thing we had to do was wait on God to get some more specific direction. We knew we were to go on television, but we had no idea how to go about it. I sincerely mean that; we did not have the slightest idea where to begin.

We found out, from talking with others who had experience in this area, that we needed a producer, so we waited for God to lead us. He reminded us that a man who was currently producing a television program for another ministry had submitted an application to us just a few months earlier.

At the time the man submitted his application we just said, "File it. We aren't on television. What would we need with a television producer?"

God knew what we did not know, and He was providing for His plan before we even knew what it was.

So we hired the producer, then he began to research equipment packages, and we waited for all that information to come in.

In the meantime, we had shared with our partners and friends what God was leading us to do. We had asked them to give toward it, and we were waiting for the money to come in. We finally got our equipment, and then realized we needed cameramen to go on the road with us and film, so we waited for God to provide them.

Then we started trying to get on television stations. The station managers told us we needed a "pilot" program — a sample of what our program would be like, so we waited for that to be finished. Then we started sending it to the stations and waiting to see if they liked it.

Finally, we went on television — a few stations at first — and waited to see what kind of response we would get.

I hope you can see from this that each phase requires waiting, especially as we leave one phase that is established and move on to the next. Waiting is a fact of life, **So be patient, brethren, [as you wait]...** (James 5:7). Notice that this verse does not say, "Be patient *if* you have to wait."

Learn To "Wait Properly"

Not only must we learn to wait on God, but we find that we must wait on people. We must learn to be patient with life, with people, with systems, with traffic and with many other things.

I can well remember when God was training me in the grocery store checkout lines, but I did not know it was training for my future.

For about a two-year period, every line I got in had either a slow clerk, a new clerk in training, a person in front of me who had items with no prices, a cash register that ran out of change and had to be replenished, or a change in shifts so I had to wait while the clerks balanced out the register.

In those situations, I would do what anyone would do — get in the shortest lines — but they always seemed to take the longest.

I believe there is a message for us there. In the natural, we are always going to choose what looks like the shortest route, but it does not always turn out to be the best one.

I could even pray about which line to get in, and still end up in the one with the most trouble.

For a long time, I would be frustrated, upset, aggravated, angry, and not doing a very good job of hiding my feelings. This display of a lack of self-control only made me look foolish, and I am sure, made the clerk (who was probably already feeling insecure), feel even worse.

I obviously did not need to have a national radio and television ministry — and be known and recognized by many — as long as my behavior was that impatient. As long as I could not even "wait properly" in a grocery store checkout line, I certainly would not be able to wait on the other things that would be necessary to see the fullness of God's plan.

Yes, very often God starts with the little things that seem of no consequence to us, but are actually very important. You see, it is a principle: If we are patient, it will show up everywhere. And if we are not patient, it will show up everywhere. God can't take a chance on us until His character has been established in us. We are His representatives — His ambassadors (2 Cor. 5:20) — and we are to give Him glory and bear good fruit.

Recently, I was in a store during the Christmas shopping season, and I waited a very long time to pay for one little item. The people in front of me had stacks of items, and it would have been very nice to be allowed to go ahead of them, but it did not happen.

I even had the experience of being overlooked once, and someone else was taken in front of me. Several ladies were waiting on customers, and when it finally came to be my turn, the lady said promptly, "Thank you for waiting. Are you who I think you are? Are you that lady on television?"

Then she said, "I thought the minute you walked in the door that you were her."

Now what if I had been acting improperly, behaving impatiently or getting angry because I was not served in proper order?

Believe me, I see many things now that I did not see while I was on the potter's wheel — while God was reshaping my attitudes and developing the fruit of His

Spirit in me. Of course, I still make mistakes, but I always let out a sigh of relief when I have been in a pressure situation and God has given me the grace to behave properly, and then I discover that someone standing around had recognized me as "the lady who preaches on television."

I remember another situation when my entire family was in a restaurant eating, and the waitress tripped and dumped an entire tray of water, coffee and tea onto my husband. He was so kind and patient with her. He even talked with the manager to make sure the waitress did not get in any trouble. She had only been working there two weeks, and she was crying.

The restaurant was very crowded, and it was her first really big table to wait on. I am sure each of us can sense how she felt. She returned later with another tray of drinks, and as she leaned across the table to where I was sitting, she said, "I think I'm nervous because you're in here. I watch you on television all the time."

My heart rose up within me, "Oh, thank You, God. Thank You, thank You, thank You, that we did not act badly in this test."

We must realize how hurt others can be by our impatient behavior, and how it can adversely affect our witness.

Hurrying Steals Joy

God has spent a lot of time teaching me that hurrying steals joy. Because He is not in a hurry, or, we might say, He does not have a "hurry up" spirit about Him, neither should we. After all, we are created in His image.

Can you imagine Jesus behaving the way we do? I doubt that He got up in the morning and began telling the disciples to hurry up and get ready so they could get on over to Jerusalem and hold a conference.

Not only does God have a timing concerning when we will see the manifestations we are waiting for, but I also believe there is a timing that we are to live in. Perhaps I should say, a speed at which we are to live. It should show up in our pace in life. How we walk, talk and eat reveals something about our attitude toward waiting.

There is a pace that is comfortable to walk at, but the "hurry up" spirit that prevails in the earth today makes us want to rush and do things that don't even require rushing. Some people talk so fast you can hardly take in and digest what they are saying. Others become irritated if you don't understand them immediately, and asking them to repeat or explain usually draws their wrath.

Many people don't really eat, they devour their food. Sometimes people who eat too fast have problems with overeating. I believe there is an emotional satisfaction that we obtain from eating. Not only do our bodies need the nourishment, but we are to enjoy our meals. If we take time to enjoy them thoroughly, we may find that we are more satisfied and require less food.

People are just generally in a hurry. So often today when we ask others how they are, they respond with, "Busy." That automatically makes me feel rushed. I get the impression that they wish I hadn't stopped them even to inquire, that I had left them alone. Most people are definitely living life in the fast lane, but it is not the lane in which we would find Jesus if He were living in the flesh on the earth today.

Make a decision not to live your life in a hurry. You won't enjoy it if you rush through it. Everything will go by in a blur.

Often people complain about how busy they are — how tired they are — but they don't do anything about it.

Make a decision! Taste of life! Savor the flavor of each day. Take some time each evening to ponder the day's events, especially the little special things that happened.

Meditate on the things that brought you joy, and you can have the pleasure of enjoying them all over again. If you are going to have to hurry all the time in order to do what you are doing, make a decision to do less.

Is getting out of your house in the morning on time a nightmare of rushing and frustration? Make a decision to do less, or get up earlier. Declare war on the spirit of "hurry up"!

Too often we are either overcommitted or under-committed. What we really need is balanced commitments. God is not impressed with our excessive activity, even when it is done in His name. Remember that peace leads to joy. If Satan can steal our peace, then he will also get our joy.

Let Patience Have Her Perfect Work

But let endurance and steadfastness and patience have full play and do a thorough work, so that you may be [people] perfectly and fully developed [with no defects], lacking in nothing.

James 1:4

When patience is fully developed in us, Satan cannot control us emotionally. This is why he fights so hard against the development of this particular fruit.

Humility is said to be the cardinal virtue out of which all the others grow. Patience is closely related to humility. As a matter of fact, I teach that impatience is pride. Impatience says, "I am far too important to have to wait." Or, "I have my plan, I'm on the move and I don't want anyone getting in my way."

James said that when patience has had her complete work in us, we will be perfect and entire — lacking in nothing. By then we will have grown enough to be out of the range of being able to be controlled by Satan, or by his work through circumstances or irritable people.

Don't despise the events in life that work patience — things that cause you to have to "wait well." They are friends, not enemies. They are helping you get where you are going. Their purpose is to help you get there with joy.

If you are in God's waiting room, which I am sure you are if you are like the rest of us, have a seat. Enjoy the wait! Don't be in such a hurry. It will only make you miserable, not anyone else. God has provided for you to have an enjoyable wait. Relax and enter in to His joy!

12

Freedom in Relationships

For you, brethren, were [indeed] called to freedom....

Galatians 5:13

Concerning the matter of enjoying life, we are all at different places in the road. Some enjoy life thoroughly, others not at all. Some enjoy it a little, and some have never even realized that they should enjoy life thoroughly.

We want to remember at this point what I have shared previously. Jesus said that He came that we might have and enjoy life, and that we might have it in abundance — to the full until it overflows. (John 10:10.) We are commanded to enjoy our lives, at least that is the way I have decided to look at it.

To enjoy life we must have liberty, and we must allow others to have liberty.

Some of the hardest work a person can take on is the job of trying to control everybody around him.

I spent a lot of years trying to control my husband, my children and my friends. I was not doing it because I was mean. As a child, I had been abused and controlled myself, and I think somewhere along the way, I decided it was either control or be controlled. I was afraid to let others lead because I felt that if I did I would never get anything I wanted.

My experience had been that anyone who had any authority in my life had hurt me, and I was not going to let that happen again. I did not really even understand that I was a controller — that I had become the very thing I hated.

I did understand that I was not happy. I had no peace and joy, and I surely was not enjoying my life. I knew I had a problem, but I did not know what it was or how to fix it.

I have been sharing chapter by chapter, things that God has shown me during my own recovery, and this chapter is no exception. This is something I have learned that has immensely helped me to enjoy my life and all the people in it.

Not only did I have a problem with attempting to control others, but in certain ways, I allowed people to control me. I was overly concerned about what they thought. I tried to live up to their expectations and silent demands.

This was the case especially among groups of people with whom I desired to be in relationship. I wanted to be a part, but was still on the outside looking in. It seems to me now as I look back, that I tried to control those who loved me, and lived in the fear of rejection of the people whose love I desperately wanted. As a result, I allowed them to steal my liberty.

God did not create us for any kind of control except self-control. We are to willingly give Him the reins to our lives, not try to keep them, nor give them to people who want to use us for their own benefit and advantage.

I have come a long way, and I believe I have been able to help a lot of people along the way. I am free to be me, and I am free from the need to control others.

Be Transformed, Not Conformed

Do not be conformed to this world (this age), [fashioned after and adapted to its external, superficial customs], but be transformed (changed) by the [entire]

renewal of your mind [by its new ideals and its new attitude], so that you may prove [for yourselves] what is the good and acceptable and perfect will of God, even the thing which is good and acceptable and perfect [in His sight for you].

Romans 12:2

God's will for us is transformation, which takes place from the inside out, not conformation, which is someone's external, superficial idea of what we should be, nor our own efforts to conform to their ideas, expectations and demands.

Often the world wants to draw the borders of a box for us and put us in it. The problem is, the box is their design, not God's.

I can never be happy and fulfilled living in someone else's box, and neither can you.

Most people think we should do what they are doing — be part of their plan. This is wonderful if God agrees, but when God says no, we must learn to say no. We must also learn to say yes when He says yes.

People have expertly developed methods of saying in a round-about way, "If you don't do what we want you to do, then we will reject you." Parents say it to their children, wives say it to husbands and husbands say it to wives. Congregations say it to their pastors. Friends say it to friends. It exists widely in every type of relationship.

The pain of rejection is hard to bear; therefore, we are very tempted to simply comply rather than to stand for our freedom. We can quickly become men-pleasers instead of God-pleasers. (Eph. 6:6 KJV.) Then we are not happy. There is no peace and no joy. We are not enjoying anything, and often we don't even know why.

We must be led by the Spirit if we are to enjoy the journey. We cannot be led by our friends and relatives.

Sometimes when we finally see that someone has been controlling us, we get very angry with that person, and all the years of our lives he or she has stolen from us. God had to show me, when I was in the anger stage, that it was just as much my fault as the other person's.

Nobody can control us if we do not permit it. Sometimes we are so tense and fearful around others — so concerned that we won't impress them — that it makes us totally miserable. It also steals our confidence and keeps the gifts of God that are in us from coming forth.

One night before one of our conferences, I went to the prayer room and found my worship leader doing stretching exercises. I thought to myself, "Now what's he doing? He's supposed to be getting ready to lead worship."

He saw me looking at him and said, "The Lord told me today when I was preparing for tonight to be loose." What he said struck me because I was teaching on liberty that night, and the first definition I had found in my study for the word "liberty," was to be loose!

When you get around other people, whether it is people you know or don't know, resist the temptation to be tense. Just relax, and loosen up. Be free to be yourself. If your friends will not allow you to be yourself, are they really your friends?

God was saying to Chris, our worship leader, "Don't feel pressured to perform."

The thief comes to kill. (John 10:10.) What does he desire to kill? The life force in us. He wants to stifle and suffocate it with fear and insecurities.

We talked at length earlier in the book about legalism and how if we live under the Law, it steals the life from us. The letter kills, but the Spirit gives life. (2 Cor. 3:6.) If we are not careful, we can allow other people to become a law to us.

Free From Comparisons

Therefore let us not judge one another anymore, but rather resolve this, not to put a stumbling block or a cause to fall in our brother's way.

Romans 14:13 NKJV

There are many things that each of us cannot do, but there are also numerous things we can do, and do well. We don't have to compare ourselves or our abilities and achievements with other people or their talents or accomplishments. We are free to be individuals. God has an individual plan for each of our lives.

Some of our lives will intermingle together, but each of us must have the liberty to be led by God. We even have the right to make our own mistakes and learn from them.

God told me once, "Joyce, just because you're right does not give you the right to cram the right thing down everyone else's throat."

Even God allows people the right of free choice, and we must maintain our right in that area, in addition to being certain that we are not party to stealing someone else's right.

I finally discovered that I did not have to be like my husband who has many wonderful qualities. I did not have to be like my pastor's wife, or my next door neighbor or the lady at church who seems to have it all together.

We allow other people to become a law to us, thinking we must be what they are. It steals our freedom, and it's no one's fault but our own.

You don't have to compare your prayer life to another person's or your Bible study habits to someone else's. As long as you feel sure in your heart that you are doing what God is leading you to do, that is all you are required to do.

When I think of the word "liberty," I sense *life*. When people preach liberty to me, I feel *life*. When legalism is preached, I sense *death*.

191

We want to please people and make them happy. It's not that this is wrong, but that it can lead to wrong.

It is scriptural to try to live in harmony with others and in peace with everyone. (Rom. 12:16,18.) Just make sure that your desire to please does not cross over the line and lead you into a controlling relationship.

Remember, when you give up your freedom, you also give up your joy.

Live and Let Live

"Live and let live," is a phrase that was designed to say, "Let's all be free." It means, "You mind your business, and I'll mind mine — and vice versa."

Did you know that even the Bible tells us that we should mind our own business?

> ...make it your ambition and definitely endeavor to live quietly and peacefully, to *mind your own affairs*, and to work with your hands....
>
> 1 Thessalonians 4:11

This is something we must endeavor to do. It should be our ambition to mind our own business.

I have definitely discovered that the application of this principle aids me greatly in enjoying my life.

Many times we get into things that were really none of our business to begin with, and those very things make us miserable. There is no anointing on us to handle someone else's affairs. That is why things get so messy when we get involved where we should not be. There is obviously a place to get involved and help someone in need, but there is also the balance line that should be honored.

My husband and I have three children who are married, and I can tell you for sure that if parents don't learn to stay out of the affairs of their adult children, it steals everyone's joy. Advice can be offered if not offered too freely, but as soon as there is any sign of that advice being rejected, the wise person backs off immediately.

We have a lot of employees at Life In The Word, and we care about our people. We want to help them whenever we can, but I learned a long time ago that I cannot be intricately involved in all their personal lives and problems. I believe a lack of balance in this area ruins many relationships with great potential.

I encourage you not to become "entangled" with the lives of others. Be a good friend, but beware of entanglements. It is possible to lose yourself in someone else's life.

I have come to the place where I feel that I have enough business of my own to mind, without getting involved in other people's.

It is amazing how our joy and enjoyment can increase just by following this one simple principle. I am very much in favor of the gifts of the Spirit, and a word in due season can really encourage and help us press forward.

Just be sure if you have a "word" for someone that it is a word from God and not a word from you. Even the precious gifts of the Holy Spirit have been abused, and people have used them to manipulate and control.

When someone gives you a word from God, always remember that you should "bear witness," that is, that you should verify it for yourself. It should be a confirmation of what the Lord has already shown you. If it is news to you, put it on a shelf and wait to see what God shows you about it.

Nosiness is another problem that must be avoided. It is one I definitely had in the past, and one that adversely affected my joy. I want you to know that I feel very strongly about this issue. Please pay close attention with your heart and be very open to God.

I am not trying to be insulting or accusing, but I feel I must exhort you: If you have difficulty minding your own business, start praying for deliverance. Make a decision to change, and it will increase your personal enjoyment greatly.

God has shown me that giving other people liberty is sowing good seeds for our own freedom in relationships. Because of our different personalities, we handle things differently, see things differently and are affected in different ways by them.

I can be in a group of people, spill a glass of water and make a mess. One personality will quickly come to my rescue with ample towels to clean up the mess. That personality will sympathize with me, knowing I am embarrassed.

Another personality may promptly want to instruct me in how I could have avoided the accident had I been more careful.

Yet another may laugh and think the whole incident is hilarious.

I could get angry or offended by two of these personalities, or I could just give them liberty to be who they are and know that if they need changing, God is big enough to take care of it. I can pray for them, but I cannot be judgmental.

Train Up a Child

Train up a child in the way he should go [and in keeping with his individual gift or bent], and when he is old he will not depart from it.

Proverbs 22:6

We must train our children. It is our responsibility before God to do so. Knowing their different personalities helps a great deal in doing it properly. When we compare the younger to the older, saying things like, "Why can't you get good grades like your sister?" and a variety of other things, we may be messing in God's business. He created each of our children and put them together for His purpose, not for ours.

Many parents want to fulfill their own unfulfilled dreams through their children, which creates a lot of pressure. Children naturally want to please their parents, but controlling parents will end up with rebellious children.

We must teach our young children what is right, but as they get older, we must also allow them to make their own choices. This will help develop a relationship of respect. They will not only respect us as their parents, but also our values, and ultimately will be more willing to follow those values.

We human beings are simply not built for outside control, and when it is forced on us, it creates problems.

When my daughters were growing up, I had certain ideas, certain standards, of what *I* thought a clean house should be. I tried to teach my girls to be clean and tidy.

One of them had a personality that did not seem to mind messes, while the other one was even more tidy than I was. I fought with the one and thought the other went a little overboard. Both grew up and now have homes of their own.

All three of us have varying definitions for the word "clean." One of my daughters is a little looser in her attitude. She enjoys her home — and it is clean — but she doesn't mind things lying around. She's the one who lives in it, so she is free to keep it as she sees fit.

The other daughter is fairly strict about how she wants things to look, but she is the one who cleans it, so that is her business.

I am probably somewhere between the two. I like my house to be a little more organized than my one daughter's, but it does not have to be as organized as the other's.

I realize now, that I lost a lot of enjoyment when the girls were growing up because I was trying to make them be like me.

In order to give people liberty, we must realize they will never be good at being anyone other than themselves.

I struggled mightily with my older son when he was growing up, and I never knew until a few years ago that we struggled because we have identical personalities — both very strong. I felt that he was always resisting everything I said or did. I thought he was just rebellious, and his attitude did grow into a form of rebellion.

However, had I known how to give him some liberty (and I might add that strong-willed children need even more freedom than other types), we could have avoided a lot of turmoil between us. My strong personality and his were working against each other, but now through Christ (and both of us learning balance), we work together all the time in the ministry.

God once told me, "Lighten up on your kids, Joyce."

I want to encourage you not to be overly rigid with your children. They have not had time to learn what you know. Give them some time, and you will be surprised what God will teach them.

We cannot make our children love God, or make them want to do right. Naturally we must correct them, but we should avoid controlling them. We should bring correction when we are led by the Spirit — not by our flesh.

I have found with our children, our employees or anyone over whom I have any measure of authority, if I correct when I really need to, and not just when I want to, the results are much better.

We should be sensitive to God in this area, just like any other, not doing what we feel like doing, but what we are truly led by Him to do. When we stop trying to run the world — stop trying to be the great choir director of life — it leaves us time to enjoy life.

Concentrate on your own freedom and maintain it before God. And give others the liberty to live their own lives. You will find an increase in your enjoyment.

My children have all turned out fine, but I missed a lot of years of enjoyment because I was intent on trying to change them when I should have been enjoying them.

People are all headed somewhere. Let's enjoy them while they make the trip. Let's enjoy where they are, while they're on the way to their destination.

When your child is two, don't wish he was three. When he is a toddler, don't wish he was in school. Don't keep looking for that "perfect" time in life when absolutely every circumstance concerning that individual will be just right. Enjoy him where he is. Each phase is part of the whole.

God has given us relationships for enjoyment, not for torment.

Make a decision today that you are going to enjoy yourself and all the people that God has placed in your life. Don't just look at what is wrong with you, or with them. Be positive, look for the good things and magnify them.

13
Don't Poison Your Joy

For let him who wants to enjoy life and see good
days [good — whether apparent or not] keep his tongue
free from evil and his lips from guile (treachery, deceit).
1 Peter 3:10

The born-again child of God has joy resident in his
spirit. It is possible, however, to poison that joy.

The Scripture quoted above says that if we want to
enjoy our lives, which is possible even if there is no apparent
reason to enjoy it, then we must keep our tongues free from
evil.

I believe the instruction is a personal one: *You* keep *your*
tongue free from evil.

When *The Amplified Bible* says that we can enjoy life
(whether apparent or not), I think it means that if we keep our
mouths positive during difficulties, though it may look to
everyone else that our circumstance should make us
miserable, we can drink joy from the fountain of our own lips.

The Fountain of Blessings and Curses

...the human tongue can be tamed by no man. It is a
restless (undisciplined, irreconcilable) evil, full of
deadly poison.

With it we bless the Lord and Father, and with it we
curse men who were made in God's likeness!

Out of the same mouth come forth blessing and
cursing. These things, my brethren, ought not to be so.

**Does a fountain send forth [simultaneously] from
the same opening fresh water and bitter?**

James 3:8-11

We can bless ourselves or curse ourselves by the way
we speak. When we bless, we speak well of; when we curse,
we speak evil of. You and I can bless our own lives and
bring joy to them, or we can curse them and bring misery
upon ourselves, by the words of our mouth.

We should be much more concerned about what comes
out of our mouths about ourselves than we ever are about
what others are saying about us. There is a well of good
things inside of us — one of them being joy. We can pull it
up and splash it all over ourselves through proper speaking.

The Bible says the human tongue can be tamed by no
man, so we will need God's help and plenty of it, to keep
the tongue under control.

In James 3:6 we read that **...the tongue is a fire. [The
tongue is a] world of wickedness set among our members,
contaminating and depraving the whole body....**

It is amazing to stop and realize all the trouble that one
tiny member of the body has created in each of our lives.
The tongue can ruin a relationship. It can usher in
depression. It can wound a friend, or, through rudeness,
hurt someone we barely know.

Verse 8 in James 3 goes on to say that the tongue is
**...restless, (undisciplined, irreconcilable) evil, full of
deadly poison.** Hmmmmm. Has your joy been poisoned?

If so, consider these Scriptures:

**The words of a whisperer or slanderer are like
dainty morsels or words of sport [to some, but to others
are like deadly wounds]; and they go down into the
innermost parts of the body [or of the victim's nature].**

Proverbs 26:22

Death and life are in the power of the tongue, and
they who indulge in it shall eat the fruit of it [for death
or life].

Proverbs 18:21

Both of these Scriptures partially express the message I
am trying to convey in this chapter: Words can help us or
hurt us, as well as the other people we are involved with.

The Tongue in Trials

The reverent fear and worshipful awe of the Lord
[includes] the hatred of evil; pride, arrogance, the evil
way, and perverted and twisted speech I hate.

Proverbs 8:13

When we are having a hard time — tribulation —what
does the tongue like to do? Talk about it! Blame it on
somebody. It likes to complain. But more than anything, it
just likes to talk about the problem (which usually doesn't
do anyone any good).

Temptations that come during trials and tribulations are
designed to drag you away from God. Talk about God —
not the problem — and you will be strengthened instead of
weakened.

Tribulation is part of life. When you own a car, you will
occasionally need to replace some of its parts. When you
own a home, you will probably need to paint it sometime or
have some other repair work done. These things are just
part of life.

We live in the world. The devil is in the world. Part of
what he does is bring tribulation. He hopes tribulation will
irritate us and steal our peace and joy.

*Satan does not want us to enjoy God or the life He has
provided for us!*

We make a big deal out of our tribulations, and are often
guilty of making mountains out of molehills. God is greater
than our problems.

I used to make such a big deal out of my problems that I made them seem bigger than they were. Dave, on the other hand, paid little attention to them at all. To him, they seemed much smaller than they did to me. Anyone who has a weakness in this area will have to grow, or he will never consistently enjoy his life.

Our worship leader, Chris, was relating to me how he had overheard some people talking about all their trials. He wondered to himself (and at the same time posed the question to God), "Why don't I have trouble any more?" Everything seemed to be fairly calm in his life at the time.

As he thought about it, he realized that one of his kids was sick, an appliance had broken down and something had happened to his car. The difference was he did not have his mind and mouth on the problems. He was busy in the ministry, traveling with us, leading worship, working at the office, writing new songs, being a good husband and father. He was busy doing what God had called him to do, which freed the Lord to do what He is supposed to do.

God wants to give us peace in the midst of the storm, while He is driving the clouds away and ushering in the sunshine.

The Bible encourages us to give a good report. (Phil. 4:8 KJV.) In Numbers 13, we see a classic example. Twelve spies were sent into the Promised Land to spy it out. Ten came back with what the *King James Version* calls an "evil report." (v. 32.) They told of the giants in the land! There were good things to report on, but they centered in on the giants.

You and I are to give a good report — talk about the positive things in life. The more we talk about good things, the more uplifted we will feel. If we choose to talk of negative things, we will feel heavy and drained. The words that go out of our mouths run alongside our faces and fall back down into our own ears as well as into other people's.

Giving an "evil report" — gossiping, slandering, complaining, backbiting — all of these things make us unhappy. Many people don't realize this fact, and others probably would not want to believe it, but it is true. Sometimes people literally get "addicted" to evil speaking. Evil speaking includes all the negative things that are mentioned in this chapter.

At one time in my life, I was so negative that if I said anything positive, it was surprising to everyone. Now I am just the opposite. I guess I am like a person addicted to drugs. Once he is set free of them, he hates them with the same passion he used to love them before his deliverance.

Once I saw the devastation of negativism and other forms of evil speaking, I hated them. According to Proverbs 8:13 God hates perverted and twisted speech. So should we. If we will be submissive to the Holy Spirit, He will prompt us to say the right things. He will also convict us when we are talking wrong. But we have to choose to cooperate with Him. He is sent to keep us on the narrow path that leads the way to life.

Agree With God, Not With the Trials

Do two walk together except they make an appointment and have agreed?

Amos 3:3

God has a good plan for our lives, and we need to bring our mouth into agreement with Him. If we go around saying things like, "Nothing good ever happens to me; all I ever have is trouble," we can expect that trouble to multiply in our lives.

Words are seeds. What we speak, we sow, and what we sow, we reap!

Begin to say, "I've got a future, and there's hope for me. God is on my side. No matter how many disappointments I have had in the past, this is a new day. Goodness and mercy are following me today."

Talking like this will help you enjoy the journey. However long you have to wait for your breakthrough, you may as well make it as enjoyable as possible.

Sometimes we are waiting for God or others to do for us what God has given us the ability and responsibility to do for ourselves. We can increase our joy through the simple principle of right speaking.

Sometimes what we say about our problems is a bigger problem than the problem. When we continually think and speak about our problems, we are making mental and verbal lists that we cannot get away from. They become prevalent in our souls. Our souls get full of the problem. God never intended our problems to get in us. They may be all around us, but were never intended to be in us. If we keep our souls full of Him and His Word, joy remains. But we can poison our joy easily and quickly by not adhering to God's principles.

I once purposely kept a list of tribulations that came my way while I was preparing to teach along these lines. We had combined a Miami, Florida, teaching engagement with a few days' vacation. We were out of town for seven days, and during those seven days, nine things happened to us that came under the category of tribulations.

Had I not written them down, I don't think I could have even remembered most of them by the time I returned home because I am no longer addicted to talking about my tribulations. I have found something better to talk about. I know for a fact that talking about them usually only increases them.

Dave played golf and his game was rained out after only six holes. He had packed his clubs and traveled to Florida with them, paid the green fee, done everything necessary to prepare for a round of golf, and then it had rained on him. Now that might not sound like much to you and me, but to a golfer, it is tribulation.

Tribulation is just all the "stuff" that goes on in an individual's life that is disappointing or irritating.

When we got to Miami, the church had arranged for us to stay at a nice hotel right on the beach, but the hotel had booked us into one room for two days and then wanted to move us to another part of the building for the rest of the stay.

This caused us to have to pack and unpack twice, more than we wanted to have to deal with. The second room we were assigned to was right next to the garbage bin, and something was stuck in it. The odor that was bleeding through the walls of our room was so bad that, at one o'clock in the morning, we were trying to find someone to come and take care of it. We discovered that hotels are not very heavily staffed at that time of night.

At our first meeting, the local power company had blocked off the parking lot. They were tearing up the street in front of the church, and people could not find places to park. While we were there, we did a marriage seminar. During the seminar, a man put fliers on the cars in the parking lot advertising for a wife.

Dave went to the church to sell tapes and could not give anyone change because I had his money pouch in my purse. Two different times the people who were picking me up to take me to the church were late. And, to top it all off, someone hit our rental car while it was parked in the garage.

Now, there was a time when I would have come back home feeling that the trip had been a disaster! But it would have been so because I had magnified the trouble by talking about it too much. As it happened, the things that went wrong really didn't bother me all that much.

Keep yourself happy by being careful about what comes out of your mouth.

Have you complained today? That will decrease your joy quickly.

Some people are "chronically critical."

Have you said negative and judgmental things about someone else? That will certainly poison your joy.

Unkind comments about other people cause us much more trouble than we know.

I was having some trouble one time with the anointing on my life. I felt something was hindering or blocking me. It was hard to explain, but something just was not right. This feeling persisted for about three weeks, and I finally knew I needed an answer from God.

He showed me that I had made a comment about another minister's preaching. I had said that it did not have any continuity to it — that he jumped all over the place. I had offended the Holy Spirit. This brother was a servant of God, preaching through the leading of the Holy Spirit, and I was judging his style.

We judge what is different, and usually because it challenges us. If this man's style was correct, maybe mine needed improvement. I did not consciously think that, but I do believe that often those fears about ourselves are the root of judgments brought against others.

I learned an important lesson from that incident. God really dealt very severely with me concerning this issue, and I know that part of the reason is because I am a teacher of His Word. He does not want bitter water coming out of the fountain one time, and sweet water the next time. He does not want me to praise Him, and curse those made in His image.

Keeping quiet about what we think we observe as faults in other people shows humility. The Bible says in Romans 12:3 that we are not to think more highly of ourselves than we ought to, but we are to realize that what we can do well is because of the grace of God.

Perhaps another person does not have the same grace gifts that you or I do. We cannot criticize others for not having something which God did not choose to bestow upon them.

Sometimes we judge people for being slower than we are, and yet God puts different speeds on all of us.

My oldest son can work faster than anyone I know, and he has had to learn that everyone is not as fast as he is. His speed, with accuracy, is a gift from God.

I am probably average when it comes to speed in getting things done. I know people who are faster than I am, but I also know people who are slower than I am.

The bottom line is, we cannot be accountable for something that God did not give us. We can learn and grow, but we will never do everything the same. Judgment comes from looking at ourselves — especially our gifts and talents — and deciding that anyone who does not do things the way we do them has a fault.

To have these kinds of things in our heart and then in our mouth is to poison our joy level. There are volumes that could be written about the mouth, but I pray that I have made my point.

Remember, **Death and life are in the power of the tongue, and those who indulge in it shall eat the fruit thereof** (Prov. 18:21). Therefore, keep your words sweet so that their fruit is sweet!

Conclusion: Finish Your Course With Joy

> But none of these things move me; neither do I esteem my life dear to myself, if only I may finish my course with joy....
>
> **Acts 20:24**

The Bible is full of Scriptures about joy, rejoicing, gladness and singing. One of my favorites is Psalm 100:1,2:

> **Make a *joyful* noise to the Lord, all you lands!**
>
> **Serve the Lord with *gladness*! Come before His presence with *singing*!**

Serving the Lord with gladness is a good goal for all of us. Often, we think we must do something great, and we forget the simple things that obviously bless the Lord. It means a great deal to Him that His children serve Him with gladness.

There were many years when I had a ministry, but not much joy. I have since learned that the Lord would rather have me glad than successful, unless I can be both.

For some time now in my meetings I have been asking people who are in full-time ministry but who are not enjoying their ministry to come to the altar for prayer. I have been astonished at how many come forward each time that altar call is made.

So many people are headed somewhere, but how many are enjoying the trip? It would be a great tragedy indeed to arrive and realize that the journey had not been enjoyed completely.

I agree with the Apostle Paul, I want to finish my course *with joy*. This particular verse seems to speak deeply to my soul. What an awesome goal: to serve the Lord with gladness, and to complete our course with joy.

Since I am the determined type, I have always been determined to complete my course. But in the past few years I have added something extra to my original goal. Now, I not only want to complete my course, but I want to complete it *with joy*.

I pray that you feel the same way. Whatever your present station in life, whatever you are called to do, wherever you are called to go, enjoy the journey. Don't waste one day of the precious life God has given you.

Rejoice in the Lord, and again I say, *rejoice!*

References

Some Scripture quotations marked Ben Campbell Johnson Paraphrase are taken from *Luke and John, An Interpretive Paraphrase* by Ben Campbell Johnson, © 1980, A Great Love, Inc., Toccoa, Georgia 30577.

Some Scripture quotations marked Ben Campbell Johnson Paraphrase are taken from *Matthew and Mark, A Relational Paraphrase* by Ben Campbell Johnson, © 1978, A Great Love, Inc., Toccoa, Georgia 30577.

Some Scripture quotations marked Ben Campbell Johnson Paraphrase are taken from *The Heart of Paul, Biblical Truth in Today's Language* by Ben Campbell Johnson, © 1976, A Great Love, Inc., Toccoa, Georgia 30577.

Scripture quotations marked KJV are taken from the *King James Version* of the Bible.

Scripture quotations marked NKJV are taken from *The New King James Version* of the Bible. Copyright © 1979, 1980, 1982 by Thomas Nelson, Inc., Publishers.

Bibliography

Exley, Richard. *Rhythm of Life*. Tulsa: Honor Books, 1987.

Strong, Dr. James. *The New Strong's Exhaustive Concordance of the Bible*. Nashville: Thomas Nelson Publishers, 1990.

Vine, W. E., Unger, Merrill F., and White, William Jr. *Vine's Complete Expository Dictionary of Old and New Testament Words*. Nashville: Thomas Nelson, Inc., Publishers, 1985.

Webster's Ninth New Collegiate Dictionary. Springfield, MA: Merriam-Webster, Inc., 1990.

Webster's II New College Dictionary. Boston: Houghton Mifflin Company, 1995.

Webster's II New Riverside University Dictionary. Boston: Houghton Mifflin Company, 1984, 1988, 1994.

About the Author

Joyce Meyer has been teaching the Word of God since 1976 and in full-time ministry since 1980. Previously the associate pastor at Life Christian Center in St. Louis, Missouri, she developed, coordinated, and taught a weekly meeting known as "Life In The Word." After more than five years, the Lord brought it to a conclusion, directing her to establish her own ministry and call it *"Life In The Word, Inc."*

Now, her *Life In The Word* radio and television broadcasts are seen and heard by millions across the United States and throughout the world. Joyce's teaching tapes are enjoyed internationally, and she travels extensively conducting *Life In The Word* conferences.

Joyce and her husband, Dave, the business administrator at *Life In The Word,* have been married for over 34 years. They reside in St. Louis, Missouri, and are the parents of four children. All four children are married and, along with their spouses, work with Dave and Joyce in the ministry.

Believing the call on her life is to establish believers in God's Word, Joyce says, "Jesus died to set the captives free, and far too many Christians have little or no victory in their daily lives." Finding herself in the same situation many years ago and having found freedom to live in victory through applying God's Word, Joyce goes equipped to set captives free and to exchange ashes for beauty. She believes that every person who walks in victory leads many others into victory. Her life is transparent, and her teachings are practical and can be applied in everyday life.

Joyce has taught on emotional healing and related subjects in meetings all over the country, helping multiplied thousands. She has recorded more than 200 different audiocassette albums and is the author of 38 books to help the body of Christ on various topics.

Her "Emotional Healing Package" contains over 23 hours of teaching on the subject. Albums included in this package are: "Confidence"; "Beauty for Ashes" (includes a syllabus); "Managing Your Emotions"; "Bitterness, Resentment, and Unforgiveness"; "Root of Rejection"; and a 90-minute Scripture/music tape entitled "Healing the Brokenhearted."

Joyce's "Mind Package" features five different audio tape series on the subject of the mind. They include: "Mental Strongholds and Mindsets"; "Wilderness Mentality"; "The Mind of the Flesh"; "The Wandering, Wondering Mind"; and "Mind, Mouth, Moods, and Attitudes." The package also contains Joyce's powerful book, *Battlefield of the Mind*. On the subject of love she has three tape series entitled, "Love Is..."; "Love: The Ultimate Power"; and "Loving God, Loving Yourself, and Loving Others," and a book entitled, *Reduce Me to Love*.

Write to Joyce Meyer's office for a resource catalog and further information on how to obtain the tapes you need to bring total healing to your life.

To contact the author write:
Joyce Meyer Ministries
P. O. Box 655
Fenton, Missouri 63026
or call: (636) 349-0303

Internet Address: www.joycemeyer.org

*Please include your testimony or help received from this
book when you write. Your prayer requests are welcome.*

To contact the author
in Canada, please write:
Joyce Meyer Ministries Canada, Inc.
Lambeth Box 1300
London, ON N6P 1T5
or call: (636) 349-0303

In Australia, please write:
Joyce Meyer Ministries-Australia
Locked Bag 77
Mansfield Delivery Centre
Queensland 4122
or call: (07) 3349 1200

In England, please write:
Joyce Meyer Ministries
P. O. Box 1549
Windsor
SL4 1GT
or call: 01753 831102

Books By Joyce Meyer

"Good Morning, This Is God!" Gift Book

JESUS — Name Above All Names

"Good Morning, This Is God!" Daily Calendar

Help Me — I'm Married!

Reduce Me to Love

Be Healed in Jesus' Name

How to Succeed at Being Yourself

Eat and Stay Thin

Weary Warriors, Fainting Saints

Life in the Word Journal

Life in the Word Devotional

Be Anxious for Nothing —
The Art of Casting Your Cares
and Resting in God

The Help Me! Series:
I'm Alone!
I'm Stressed! • I'm Insecure!
I'm Discouraged! • I'm Depressed!
I'm Worried! • I'm Afraid!

Don't Dread —
Overcoming the Spirit of Dread
with the Supernatural Power of God

Managing Your Emotions
Instead of Your Emotions Managing You

Healing the Brokenhearted

"Me and My Big Mouth!"

Prepare to Prosper

Do It! Afraid

*Expect a Move of God in Your Life...**Suddenly***

Enjoying Where You Are on the Way to Where You Are Going

The Most Important Decision You'll Ever Make

When, God, When?

Why, God, Why?

The Word, the Name, the Blood

Battlefield of the Mind

Battlefield of the Mind Study Guide

Tell Them I Love Them

Peace

The Root of Rejection

Beauty for Ashes

If Not for the Grace of God

By Dave Meyer

Nuggets of Life

Available from your local bookstore.

Harrison House
Tulsa, Oklahoma 74153

The Harrison House Vision

Proclaiming the truth and the power
Of the Gospel of Jesus Christ
With excellence;

Challenging Christians to
Live victoriously,
Grow spiritually,
Know God intimately.